when the SKUNKBRUSH TURNS

A MONTANA PRAIRIE REVERIE

CAL CUMIN

Kindle Direct Publishing print book (ISBN: 978-0-9987788-1-5)

Kindle Direct Publishing e-book (ISBN: 978-0-9987788-2-2)

Draft2Digital ebook (ISBN: 978-0-9987788-3-9)

Edited by Self Publishing Services LLC

Cover Design by Meld Media Montana LLC

Cover Image: Benchland" 12"x12" by Dale Livezey copyright 2018.

Formatting by Meld Media Montana LLC

To my family.

TABLE OF CONTENTS

"The Indian prefers the soft sound of the wind darting over the face of the pond, and the smell of the wind itself cleansed by a mid-day rain or scented with a pinon pine. The air is precious to the Redman. For all things share the same breath—the beasts, the trees, man. The Whiteman does not seem to notice the air he breathes. Like a man dying for many days, he is numb to the stench... What is man without the beasts? If all the beasts are gone, man would die from great loneliness of spirit, for whatever happens to the beasts also happens to man. All things are connected. Whatever befalls the earth befalls the sons of the earth."

(Attributed to Duwamish Indian Chief Seattle)

CAL CUMIN

WHEN THE SKUNKBRUSH TURNS[1]

I'VE ALWAYS THOUGHT it beautiful the way Absáaloke elders described the seasons of the year. It also seems that the colorful fall we have here in the Valley of the Yellowstone justifies a poetry of description we don't use.

Pretty Shield, Crow medicine woman, called September "the-moon-when-the-wild-plums-fall"; how evocative of this unique and short period on our Montana land.

Walking the length of the North Fork of Alkali Creek this late summer day, I realize it is "the-time-when-the-skunkbrush-turns," i.e., late September. When-the-skunkbrush-turns is a time, a place, a smell, a sight, and maybe, if I were more enlightened, a meditation on the rhythm of the Earth and the connectedness of all things.

This place is sandstone hills and dusty cow paths beside narrow trails of bitter water in a small valley. The smell is of dryness, as if the Earth is gathering and storing its summer fragrances for the long cold months of winter (the-time-when-the-Chinooks-come?). The sun and breeze carry away the remaining smells of sage and bunchgrass and pine, releasing them later in memories and dreams. There is also the ever-restless wind, and the fine, airborne sand that rests in the corner of your eyes and mouth after a long, prairie, sun-bright day.

---

1 Originally published in *The Billings Outpost*, Billings, Montana.

WHEN THE SKUNKBRUSH TURNS

Pretty Shield's language reflected a nomadic culture in which the land itself and all that was on it was part of life; not just someplace to mine, farm, or timber, or upon which to build one's latest dream house. Her words remind me of First Americans much farther north who have something like a hundred different words for snow. Even if we had a more poetic way of describing this land that nurtures us and our way of life, we probably wouldn't use a phrase like "the-time-when-leaves-are-fully-grown" to describe something more easily referred to as June. We just have other things to think about (we rationalize), plus our attention span has been trained to the thirty-pushing-for-fifteen-second sound bite of media and networking gods. The beauty and timelessness of the land is pushed aside for the really important things--those activities from which we can materially profit.

But the prairie remains there outside our cities and towns, the lion-colored hills of autumn beckoning, waiting patiently the prodigals' awareness of its gifts.

Starter castles are going up now on the south rim of the little alkali canyon, homes large enough to house third--world villages. The vertical angles, straight edges, and disparate colors break the undulations of pine, sandstone, and gentle hills. Who will be the first to project their decks out over this small and ancient valley where the meaning of pictographs of those long gone are still unknown. Whose barking dogs will be first to chase the small herd of mule deer and cringe at the nocturnal invitation of Mr. Coyote to come and play.

Nearing the Warfield Ranch, an area of big sage, *Artemisia Tridentata,* that seems unusually lush waves in the soft wind like a field of grain. Walking through the chest-high mini-grove, admiring the cadence of wind and sun and smell, I realize this hardy flagbearer of the prairie is blooming, its woody stalks heavy with tiny flowers and seeds. This could be "the-time-when-the-sagebrush-blooms." Works for me. Maybe if we combined the Latin cadence with moon time? Like the snow of the far north, Montana's prairie requires many names to capture its myriad moods and faces.

The-time-when-the-skunkbrush-turns is a fluid time. Starting in the high Beartooth Country with the sudden yellow flash of aspens and cottonwoods among the darkening pines, it moves quickly down and outward across the plains--splotching red, orange, and gold in magic places like the Sweetgrass Hills and the Wolf Mountains before slipping silently down the Blue Creek coulees into the large, lower drainages like our Yellowstone. It's not an end; it's a celebration of life in constant transition— snow, long nights, Orion, slush ice whispering on the river, and the conversation of the mighty chickadee in snow-covered breaks.

Pretty Shield also said, "Our hearts stay young if we let them."

VOICE OF THE YELLOWSTONE[2]

THE YELLOWSTONE RIVER speaks to those who listen, but most people don't hear her whispers. It's an old adage that in order to experience miracles, one has to be open to them. Her voice is such a phenomenon--quiet, elegant, pervasive, and spiritual—but also primal and powerful.

Most people can hear the slush ice moving under a full moon on dark winter nights—a busy, exotic, going-places kind of sound. Some also know the loud, freight train roar of floodwater carrying upstream downstream--unstoppable, primitive, sheer power and exuberance.

But when she's quieter, one can hear the echoes of all that has happened on her broad sparkling back: the generations of Lakota, Absáaloke, and Piegan who lived with her; the great buffalo wolves and plains grizzlies; the splash of Cavalry troopers leaving the dust of a hard day's march in the clear water of summer; the dark hour's blast of a forty-five-seventy beginning the Battle of Poker Flats; the yip of Texas drovers glad to finally reach her but dreading the crossing; the lonesome whistle of the first locomotive elbowing its way up the river's edge; the moans of Little Big Horn wounded passing quietly downstream on the steamboat *Far West;* the chunk of the woodhawk's axe.

---

2 Originally published in *Last Best News*, Billings, Montana, December 29, 2016.

There is still in the music of the river the cacophony from vast seas of buffalo boiling across her wide waters, the great bulls bellowing, calves bawling, flared nostrils blowing mist that rises with great clouds of fine gumbo dust to blur the prairie sun, the endless swarm of flies. Listen also for the dim ragged voices of the miners, land speculators, outlaws, surveyors, bushwhackers, mountain men, and—too—the laughter of generations of young enjoying her grassy banks.

Although the crescendo of noise increased greatly with the coming of the white man, the river also heard and still carries in her native heart the whispers of the ancients when the land was a vast silence, glaciers and sabertooth were her neighbors, and the bipeds few. As part of the way things work, she also recorded for those who listen the voice of the stars that have graced her proud mane in all the bright nights since she was born, a history of the universe in her flowing bounty—all that she is.

SILVER SAGE[3]

THERE IS A tall, ancient, sagebrush beside a mailbox along a road to the Yellowstone River—a remnant of open prairies long ago. A wild-looking piece of creation, it is not content to hide in the roadside debris of beer cans, accumulations of dirt and dust, and the many exotic weeds. It is silver sage, pushing its wild weathered head up four feet or more through all the seasons regardless of temperatures that can be well over a hundred degrees and as low as forty below. Some older stems lie in a bunch on the ground and lift occasionally with the wind, reminding me of some drunken, gray-headed harridan struggling to raise her head from a barroom floor for just one more swig. In its struggle to keep its place in an older order of things, the sage exudes an exotic perfume in the small sentinel space it still claims.

Numerous small hairs give the leaves their subtle gray color like the eyes of the lover my memory keeps. If I rub, ome of its narrow-pointed leaves together, I get an aromatic explosion of the basic West: of endless prairies, of antelope people, and dirt roads that disappear in wavering horizons. Most poignantly, I remember driving cattle, the hooves of horses and shorthorns trampling sage underfoot, mixing *in extremis* its aroma with sweat, dust, and wind—a memory forever captured in the anterooms of my youth. Drive across sagebrush country and,

---

3 Published in *Last Best News*, Billings, Montana, March 9, 2017.

when you stop, listen to the ticking of the heated engine and the silence of big country, and smell the essence of bruised sage that has slapped against the undercarriage.

One can burn the fine leaves for their aroma. Simply putting some on the hot surface of a wood stove creates the instant scent of sagebrush—and memories. Native Americans burn sage as a spiritual cleanser to initiate sacred or body and soul cleansing ceremonies and to honor the departed and the Creator—to obtain their attention, blessing, and cooperation with the living. The dried and twisted stems of dead sagebrush also create an almost smokeless fire—good for when you're hiding from the jihadis tracking you, or it's just you and the Sundance Kid and the damned railroad men are finally closing in.

It is mainly the white man that appraises natural systems in terms of profit, and the sagebrush does not compete well with grasses for cattle. But it is not a noxious weed, harmful or uneatable to cattle that our abuse of the land has encouraged everywhere today. It is, rather, a source of forage in fall and winter for all ungulates, particularly useful when the snow is deep and the bunch grasses sleep, buried. The hardy sage collects the drifting snow on its leeward side in countless small drifts stretching across bleak, winter prairies, and offers its hardy self to animals that need the sustenance or to smaller beings seeking shelter from bitter winds.

WHEN THE SKUNKBRUSH TURNS

Big Sagebrush, a sister species to the Silver Sage, grows taller. I am always impressed when I walk through a patch of Big Sage and find it over my head like some primitive woody gray forest. Its leaves are not pointed like Silver Sage. Rather, each leaf ends in three small lobes, and it smells just as good as the rest of the family.

If the Yellowstone River is our mother, then the great prairie stretching to distant horizons and shimmering mountains is our father. This is not pagan religion. It is just a sense of the order of things under the Creator. I remember coming back from a distant war a long time ago to the old airport terminal at Billings. Before I called anyone, I just sat in there for awhile and looked northward across the winter-flecked land to the Bull Mountains and the skies and clouds stretching clear to the once great Missouri River. Like the magic of divining rods, I let my roots sink into the Earth. My homecoming, native son to ancient father, this land I had missed so much.

ROAD TO HAILSTONE BASIN

AT THE TOP of the road traditionally known as the Hogsback that snakes up from the sprawl of west Billings, Montana, the evening sun reflects blearily off the distant snow fields of the sedate and majestic Crazy Mountains seventy miles away. Meadowlark song rules the land this May evening; their music penetrates the cab of my small, '93, Toyota pickup, even over the wailing of an old Willie Nelson cassette. Sparrow hawks watch their territory from established spaces on the paralleling power lines, and horned larks lift from the roadbed just in the nick of time. Snow is off the land, finally, and for this short period of springtime, water pools in every depression on the prairie, reflecting more light and sky than the land and sky itself. Yet, even here, Realtor signs blight the intersections of gravel roads on either side.

New houses seem to have sprung up every time I drive up onto these bench lands. The main dwelling is often rather shabby, maybe a single-wide house trailer, but alongside is a great looking shop—two or three large doors to accommodate his RVs, four-wheelers, a sorry-looking boat, and at least two snowmobiles. The pickup in the driveway is as big as he can afford; the passenger car the wife drives to work is several years older and getting worse for wear, especially considering where what's-his-face has decided to homestead.

WHEN THE SKUNKBRUSH TURNS

I pass a beautiful brown-and-white pinto that reminds me of my grandfather's love of these hardy little Indian ponies, something that got him in trouble back in the hardscrabble times.

The pavement ends at the small town of Molt. Someone else put it aptly, "Molt is where the pavement dies." In the center of town, the former post office building became the general store, and—most recently—The Prairie Winds Café, a great place for breakfast and lunch. On weekends, there was usually a wait, as live music and good food brought a crowd in from Billings. But, even with the nearby city people, there was not enough business for the small café to survive.

The road jogs north from Molt past an old and picturesque windmill that, as if remembering better times, looks forlornly out across wide prairie and farmland stretching all the way to the foothills of the mountains that form the distant horizon. I have never been able to photograph that windmill in a way that captures the feeling of it as it haunts my mind's eye; every time I drive by, it challenges me.

These dusty gravel roads tend to follow section lines and constantly turn at right angles, and, at the direction of bullet-ridden signs, I turn west, then north again.

The endless stubble of harvested wheat fields is broken only by old homesteader houses long abandoned, gray, and—leaning from the years of wind—sinking slowly into the timeless maw of the prairie. Slowly passing. Slowly changing. The land eventually endures.

The Crazies are losing the blinding white reflection off the high snow and the jagged blue-gray horizon softens as the sun moves down. Too many beer cans, bottles, and plastic everything are carried on the breast of this land. I think momentarily of inadvertently slipping off the road and into the alkali water-filled borrow ditch. Wearing Tevas and shorts, I am a city boy to whomever local might stop and help me. And I would need the help, as the mud under the stagnant water is pure gumbo grease and would swallow my truck. I owe it to that pinto-loving grandfather who homesteaded on this prairie not to embarrass myself and him by doing anything so stupid. I drive the sliding gravel curves with prudence.

The land continues to glow with the softening light of the sun now settling north of the mountains. Ducks make long rippling arcs in the still surfaces of ponds near the road. A red tail hawk struggles for altitude, carrying a vole in its claws. A northern harrier undulates low across the greasewood and sage. Crows continually seek their edge in this spare land.

To the southwest lies the Lake Basin country, a large playa or shallow lake miles across that of late only has water in the melt of spring—if then. Most of the time, it is a desert of white alkali that the wind whips into dust storms visible for miles. Finger-like escarpments may someday reveal the earliest passages of man in this area, as the lake must have been impressive thousands of years ago.

On the last turn, I stop and get out to relieve myself of some Blue Boar Beer. Later tonight, as part of the cycle of life here, a coyote will probably sniff the same spot, hose it thoroughly, and scratch and scatter the scented soil, letting fellow canines and all living things know exactly how he feels.

The land slopes away from me, covered like a fine cobweb with the settling dust kicked up by my truck. The road heads due west now from here, past Rapelje where the early railroad line from Billings ended, serving as it did the big wheat and grain farms of the era. Its rail cars once also carried tons of buffalo bones from the Six-Shooter Buffalo Jump site about fifteen miles west. I've often wondered about the many arrow and lance points mixed with those thousands of bones turning up in faraway Chicago rail yards. Ten miles from here, the road turns north once again at the Stillwater County line.

Somewhere beyond the rise behind me and completing a full-circle view, the Bull Mountains anchor the Musselshell Valley, its rich grassland the destination of Texas

trail herds that created the legend of the American cow-
boy in that sweet time of the 1880s.

Prairie dogs have built a community south of the road,
and a short burrowing owl, having privatized a prai-
rie dog burrow, sits guard-like in the middle of some
mounds. Pronghorn, that ancient and elegant race the
Crow Indians call the Antelope People, ignore me from
the gently rolling hills. The innate, subtle, earthy colors
of a roadkill porcupine are—maybe for the last time—
again beautiful in the passing golden light of evening.

As twilight comes, I enter the Hailstone National Wild-
life Refuge. This is a favorite place for people who call
themselves hunters to come and shoot prairie dogs early
in the morning. Nothing like a wildlife refuge to serve
up your soft targets. The ruts on the two-track road
are deep, the large culvert crossing of the creek below
the dam retaining wall barely functional. I prefer it this
way; it's harder to reach, to get to, to vandalize, to litter.

Topping the rise beside the crest of the spillway, the
shallow alkaline lake extends before me for a mile or so.
I'm attracted to the life in this place—and its isolation.
The water birds are the main players, seeming to party
all night, and it is the only spot I've heard meadowlarks
piercing call at two in the morning.

WHEN THE SKUNKBRUSH TURNS

I drive around the lake to a flat spot and park my truck so the back—where I'll be sleeping—faces the lake, and, later, moonrise—and, later still, tomorrow's sun.

Getting out, I lean against the truck and let my senses fan out across this special place, to wick away the city vapors, and learn once again to listen to the silence. Zen-like, the quiet of the land reveals itself. The cacophony of bird song focuses the ears. An owl circles above me for a second time, trying to figure out this sudden apparition in his evening world, eventually diving at me for a close look before going on about his nocturnal quest. The evening breeze is cool, keeping the mosquitoes at bay.

A waning half-moon finally rises yellow in the east while small clouds still catch the pink high in the sundown sky. I take a small flask of stingers and sip, thank the Creator for this incredible evening, crawl in my sleeping bag, and sleep soundly through the night, the whispers of living prairie all around me.

GOODBYE TO A SPECIAL PLACE

HUNDREDS OF YEARS ago, the artist stepped back to study the imprint of her hand on the grainy sandstone surface above her head. She was satisfied and added nothing else. The red berry dye reflected her slender hand well. As she had lifted her fingers, she had trailed them slightly upward, elongating each finger—reflecting the radiation outward of her personal power. She thought the simplicity elegant. Daubing additional pigment to provide a deep, dark, and uniform coloration, she watched the dye seep deeply into the porous sandstone as it dried.

"What does it mean, Mother?" her young son of six seasons asked.

She didn't answer him. Smiling, she merely said, "Do you like it?"

She hadn't planned to paint her hand on the smooth stone, consciously at least. Her husband was working a short distance away and higher in the sandstone cliffs that bordered the north side of this small, peaceful drainage. He was the recognized artist of the band of family and friends that made up the camp. His drawings were more complex—of the horse and the turtle and the shield-like symbol for the four forces always at work in the lives of the plains nomads: fire, wind, water, and sun.

WHEN THE SKUNKBRUSH TURNS

She took her son's hand and returned to their nearby tipi, joining her sister in grinding the dark red choke-cherries in with the dried buffalo meat. It was a pleasant summer on the plains of what would someday be a place called Montana just north of a city called Billings in a small drainage called Alkali Creek. White men, the future nemesis of this young woman's culture, were still thousands of miles to the east and several generations in her people's future.

Now, still sitting near the pictographs as quietly as I can on a red sandstone ledge in the shadow of a ponderosa pine, I watch two young coyotes amble down a small coulee below me. They seem intent on getting someplace instead of paying proper attention to their surroundings. I hoped they develop a better sense of the dangers of their world, or they won't make it in that tough and dangerous nitch between modern man and the rapidly receding natural environment in which coyotes survive.

Seeing the coyotes makes my journey here complete. The mule deer, marmot, chipmunks, jackrabbit, and the many birds are all part of this sense of place in the prairie, but it is the aura of the tough, wily, maligned coyote and of the simple rock pictographs that massage an itch in my soul.

I have been sojourning here for years. When I was a boy, I spent some summers with my grandparents who had built a small log home on Alkali Creek farther downstream. I've retained a sense of ownership in the ambling streambed, although most of the beautiful valley is now filled with homes, schools, and roadway.

Driving on the paved road extending up the canyon near the Yellowstone River, away from the busiest street in the state, fleeting memories tick by like an odometer: where I carved my initials deep in platform rock, where it had taken a long time to kill a porcupine with a bow and arrow, where Linda (the great love of my early youth) and I raced our horses.

I try not to think of when I vandalized sandstone. I don't kill anything anymore, not even spiders, and Linda married someone else. I had never had time to say good-bye to the lower canyon where all the homes are; they just seemed to be there one aware day.

The basic structure of the small canyon remains the same, however: sandstone cliffs; the soft undulation of drainage and hills; and most of the pines, skunkbrush sumac, and the great expanse of sky. In some future millennium, maybe it will return as it once was.

I walk farther on and watch from a seclusion of rock and fallen tree the quiet valley below me. The canyon's south slope is shrouded in monochrome shadow. A small herd of mule deer leisurely graze a half mile away, their dark gray shapes blending into the shaded hillside.

WHEN THE SKUNKBRUSH TURNS

It is then I first notice the uniform shape of a roofline on the far edge of the valley. Apparently started in the spring, it confronts my senses with a distant barking of a dog and the sharp rap of hammers. I know now why the animals seem scarce on this visit.

It is the beginning of an end for nature in this small remaining part of the Alkali Creek drainage.

THE QUIET

IT TAKES A while for the quiet to settle in, for the wind sounds from driving and the voices of the city to disappear. The four faithful cylinders of my old Toyota nudge quietly onto the prairie. This ancient land and the old, faithful truck seem to appreciate each other, the former probably relieved that another one at least twice as big isn't charging over the scarred trail, beer bottles scattering in the dust.

The short-eared owl sitting on the steel post out in the softness of the dry lakebed swivels his head to check me out. I remember, long ago, a mentor owl who flew low over me and clapped his wings to remind me my depression didn't count for much out here in the big open.

Pugnacious-looking little flies, about three millimeters long, seem to like the black topper on my truck. They're thick chested (large thorax?) with a small round head attached by a hair-thin neck; six skinny legs—perfectly proportioned like all insects to address their particular needs—and wings folded back into a long tail. All of them pointed into the breeze like they were waiting a signal to lift off, and none of them bothering me one iota. Small jumping things in the mishmash of grass and ground cover are probably young grasshoppers, a portent of the summer to come.

WHEN THE SKUNKBRUSH TURNS

The meadowlarks are a loud chorus of burrs, clucks, and the usual melodious song befitting of our state bird. One had to parse lesser songs from the chorus. A friend of mine firmly believes that, because the meadowlark only stays around for the nice weather, we should appoint the cocky and raucous magpie as our state bird. Wouldn't affect my appreciation of the wonderful little meadowlark but would probably better reflect the nature of things here on this high, dry land.

After a time, the quiet settles in my mind, and the softer echoes come through—the cry of the long-billed curlew, the squabbling of the shorebirds and ducks partying on the remaining water, and, finally and most listened for, the joyous yipping howls of the prairie song dog. I think the coyotes like to hype themselves up before a night of prowling. In the morning in the same kind of twilight, they often give vent again, maybe a thank you for surviving the night before once again facing a day as the most hunted of all the prairie creatures.

I had seen, driving up, silhouetted against a darkening eastern sky and intent on the vole or mouse he was about to jump, Mr. Coyote. Such a sighting is a leap bounder for me in the steps to silence. Brother predator and all.

Maybe the prairie dog comes a close second as most vilified of the small animals man likes to kill on the plains, but there's no macho complement in shooting the noisy little mutts. The justification, of course, is that they destroy valuable grassland, proliferate like the plague, and create holes in which valuable livestock break legs.

Like the urban myths we're finally acknowledging, this leg breaking thing is a rural myth. There's no documented case of a cow breaking a leg. During the 1860s and the great cattle drives when every damned thing between Texas and Montana was an obstacle, the prairie dog holes were an issue. The horrendous energy of those great herds stampeding mindlessly in the lightning-struck darkness, and the hardy drovers trying to turn them, caused or were affected by everything in their blind path—including badger and prairie dog holes, sink holes, trees, horn-gutted horses, Indians, rustlers, and everything else. (Teddy Blue in his *We Pointed Them North* probably does the best job of defining this unique and very short era in the American West.)

Today, old prairie dog towns are often where cows prefer to graze, as the grass grows there new, green, and sweet. It's been well fertilized and properly aerated, and its tender shoots are tastiest. The little dogs like the cattle because man with his killing toys usually won't shoot into a bunch of cows—usually. Burrowing owls re-use older dog holes, and the predators of sky and fang find the prairie dog villages a nice meal in a land of sparse resources. The little rodents don't need our protection, but they would sincerely appreciate being left alone.

WHEN THE SKUNKBRUSH TURNS

Brother Moon is early in his cycle and the half-face cold until I glass it. The craters of his ancient cheek proudly reflect our precious sun's light and gift it to me on this vast prairie below. When the wind hits a certain volume, the prairie grasses begin to sing, a distinctive susurration rivaling any Gregorian chant—but gentler, of course, poem-songs of joy and freedom and memory—and the prairie quiet.

BATTLE OF POKER FLATS

IT'S A HOT day, probably not unlike August 14, 1872, when, during the previous night, Lakota and Oglala Sioux, Cheyenne, and Arapaho decided to attack a U.S. Army bivouac a few miles downstream on the Yellowstone River from the Billings, Montana of today.

It was the young braves who started it all; the older and wiser men knew they didn't have enough ammunition to engage a well-equipped Army unit. One young brave snuck into the sleeping Army camp and attempted to steal a rifle leaning against a tree near its dozing owner. The latter was an old fox on the dangerous frontier and saw the attempt, shooting the warrior and arousing the whole camp; the battle started.

This is the site that some men came from all over the country to see as part of a tour led by Neil Magnum, former superintendent of the Little Bighorn Battlefield. A local historian and crusty Army veteran of a later era, Harold Hagen, explained the battlefield to the men, who had also been to the Little Big Horn and Canyon Creek battlefields as part of their tour.

This battle site is largely neglected except for the efforts of men like Hagen and the more than noteworthy caretaking of the present landowners. As a historian said recently, "All things turn on Custer!" None of this would be important without him.

The site of the Baker Battle is important for several reasons. Some historians feel it was the first skirmish that finally ended with the Battle of the Little Bighorn. Secondly, major players were involved, including Crazy Horse, the almost mythic warrior whose personae is still largely unknown and being explored, although his name is familiar to most Americans. Here in history, this young and restless warrior rode back and forth across the battlefield in front of the Army daring them to shoot him; they tried. Then there was Sitting Bull, old for a warrior by this time—and wise, as he needed to be. He knew the futility of the coming fight but was unable to control the young men in his war party. Finally Sitting Bull laid down his weapons and, taking only his pipe and tobacco, went out a hundred yards in front of his companions. There he sat down and smoked as the dust from the heavy fifty-seventy caliber bullets of the U.S. Army kicked up around him. When done with his leisurely smoke, he got up and calmly ambled back to his warriors, who now were more than willing to listen to him.

Hagen, an old 10th Special Forces Group paratrooper, is more than qualified to explain the battle. He, David Eckroth, and the Frontier Heritage Alliance have pulled together every single bit of data about the site they could find. David, a master at metal detecting, was the first to investigate the site. Because the Army had standard deployment locations during battle, he was able to determine such locations by the empty cartridges his metal detector found. Once he found the Army positions, he went to where they were probably shooting and found the bullets themselves. Each shell casing has a unique firing pattern. The Indians used a different rifle than the Army, and some of the Indian shell casings had been recycled four and five times. Little wonder Sitting Bull was concerned.

The commander of the eight troops of 2nd Cavalry and 7th Infantry was Major Eugene Baker, a battle-hardened soldier probably suffering post-traumatic stress disorder from his bloody experiences in the Civil War. He drank a lot, the only medicine available for a mental illness gotten in service to his county. He had been drinking and playing cards late the night before. So, when the shout went up, his command abilities at the time would later came into question by historians.

Two years earlier, Baker had been ordered to teach a lesson to a recalcitrant Piegan warrior who had killed a settler. It was January and forty below zero on the Marias River in northwestern Montana. Fueled by alcohol (for the cold, of course) and guided by two untrustworthy scouts, Baker attacked the wrong village. Of the one hundred and seventy-three known dead, the Blackfoot superintendent later reported that, except for fifteen men, all killed were sick or women, children, and old men; all able-bodied men had been faraway hunting buffalo.

Baker lost one man on the Marias, as he did here on the Yellowstone (Sergeant McLarren). Indian dead are unknown, but historians are sure that Indian weapons and warriors from this fight showed up later at the Little Bighorn. Baker died at forty-eight from cirrhosis of the liver.

CABIN FEVER

CABIN FEVER IN late February or just the need to get out of Dodge, the condo, my skin. The edges get rawer when the young mutant in big wheels roars up behind me and mouths his opinion of my driving. I need some Montana open space big time, and the bigger the better.

It's only when I've topped the hogsback of the Molt Road west of Billings and start the gentle drop into the Lake Basin country that I pull over and eat my super burritos—with fire sauce. Only now do I unbuckle my seat belt and my pants belt and let a winter's tension drift away through the open sunroof into the flowing prairie breeze.

The great front of the Beartooth Range spreads along the southwestern horizon, the sun shimmers off the high snowfields in sharp contrast to dark forests, shaded peaks, and hidden canyons. The Crazies sparkle to the west, proud and independent of the larger mountain ranges south across the interstate highway that slices through the Yellowstone Valley. Edging the viewshed to the north are the Snowies and to my left rear the Pryors, sharing the distance with the low-lying Bighorn range of Wyoming.

All this and only twenty minutes out of town. I shudder inwardly, remembering the three hours it once took me to escape Los Angeles. I also realize—the way Billings is sprawling—the small town of Molt I pass through is but a suburb away.

My prairie roots are out here in this vast open flatness where the curvature of the Earth and the eye's sheer inability to see mark the distance. My mind struggles to get back around the old familiar. Rapelje is a distant tumble of dark buildings, the rough edges of Big Coulee break the horizon to the north, Battle Butte squats in perennial mystery, and the lake basin's notorious alkali dust is dormant for the day. Dirty brown snowbanks line the leeward side of the gravel roads in defiance of the fifty-degree weather.

There is both artistry and a master plan working here. First, the tumbleweeds gather and line the fences. Then the snow blows and is caught by this natural snow fence, generating water in borrow ditches long after it has disappeared elsewhere on the sand and gumbo range. The ditches become the most fertile and diverse of the micro ecosystems of all the surrounding land. This growth, in turn, eventually leads the county road department to blade out the accumulated life system, and the process starts over again. There are lessons in this somewhere.

I study the occasional hawk, trying to identify late winter plumage so beautiful and proud under their fierce facades. Only by the undulating flight of the northern harrier do I at least recognize this prairie bird. The sheer size of another, uniformly dark hawk marks a mature golden sitting on the highest point it can find in this ancient lakebed—a hilltop shaped like the sand in the bottom of an hourglass.

West of Rapelje I swing off the main road and leave the farmed fields for the distant hills, the lair of dinosaur bones I used to find in my long-ago perambulations. I drive slowly, my vertically challenged Saab not used to roads where the only tire tracks predate the winter snow. There are no houses here, although the remains of old homesteads—old dreams—dot the landscape. I feel the peace of isolation revive me. I pass slowly by one lone ranch hand working to repair a small corral in the wide open; his dusty, battered pickup truck in contrast to the shiny monsters roaring around the urbs and sub-urbs. I give the polite greeting with my index finger; he barely nods. A short distance past he has disappeared, a small dot in a tan landscape in the rearview mirror.

The cottontails along the road and the occasional prairie dog subdivision point to at least a healthy predator-prey life system in the area. A range, so badly overgrazed that only the prickly pear stands out, screams for jus-tice; even the sagebrush is down to the nubs. It's prob-ably some federal range management program thing. I'm glad the cattle are now gone—along with every available living sprout, but it might be edifying to meet the person responsible; "attention" and "two-by-four" come to mind.

WHEN THE SKUNKBRUSH TURNS

Prairie grass is good, sound, open-range feed, but the natural wheatgrasses and sedges must be allowed to grow. When the native, usually drought-resistant, vegetation is as badly abused as this, the weeds come—the skeleton and knapweed. In our culture's constant search for profit regardless of short-term cost, the weeds will some day beat us, and we will have a world dominated by thistles, wild dogs, grackles, roaches and crows.

The road becomes two tracks across an open range dotted only by the fallen remains of an old wooden water tower. Its metal bands are rusting, but its bygone craftmanship, like a work of art, is still reflected in the hand-fitted boards, now loosening in abandon across the land that will slowly, almost reverently, swallow what remains. I herded cattle in this area when I was a kid, not realizing then how glamorous such work was supposed to be. Heading up into the hills on a road I haven't been on before, I keep looking for any ranch houses that might make me want to turn and scuttle back to somewhere they might not be so inclined to want to know what a three-county license plate was doing in their front yard. Entering a small canyon of exquisite beauty, the road hugs a steep hillside and the narrow walls protect naked cottonwood stands and a springtime streambed. A fat mulie doe decides to get up from her day's nesting, and, gathering a couple of friends, casually disappears into the darkness of bottom thickets.

On the crest of the ridgeline, the land drops away in all directions, south down somewhere to Columbus, west to more foothills undulating all the way to the Crazy Mountains, and down back the winding trail I've just climbed. The road in front of me still has snow drifted across it. I think I can make if I keep my speed up, but I also realize this snow swept ridge would be a hell of a place—late in the day now—to get stuck. But, with typical male bravado, I really hate to go back over ground already covered.

I speed up a little, slosh into the bank, angle for a bare spot on the high side of the trail, and move on through. Maybe it's just a land karma thing, letting me through. I've always had the feeling that nothing of nature in Montana will ever hurt me, probably a remnant of conquering such fears a long time ago, by myself and about nine years old, on these same prairies in the endless darkness of winter nights. The peace of the high prairie now rides always with me.

I finally slip back on to a more frequently traveled road, a properly maintained and official Stillwater County road judging by the depth of alien gravel recently spread on its surface. I wonder who out here has enough clout to get their road maintained in such good fashion. Perhaps the Keating Ranch. I once worked there back in the dark ages—helping my grandmother who was the ranch cook. Several ranches and farms along the dusty road have new signs proudly declaring ownership and management, seized gauntlets in the challenge of trying to make a living on these arid plains. The Keating signs are weatherbeaten, starting to splinter, the prancing horse fading.

I keep heading generally east. There are road signs at intersections now, just like in town—white on green background. I turn on one called Cadillac Hill just to see if there is any indication at all why it has that moniker. When it bends west, I turn around. I'm heading home but taking the long route, trying to avoid going back on roads I came on.

I love old fence posts and notice some classics. Old juniper posts a foot in diameter have been soldiering for a hundred years. Some are slowly rotting off and now lean in the direction of least resistance. All have the wounds of barbed wire wrapped around them, countless repairs, countless winters. Just below the gray surface of these old posts, the wood is soft red in color and beautifully aromatic.

A lot of fir posts lie along the borrow ditches. These abandoned, straight-grained, soft wood posts are common and are the greatest of fireplace starters. Cut in short lengths and finely split, these old posts provide neat and clean kindling, the kind advertised in fancy and expensive catalogues from back-East cities. The posts lie by the hundreds along the backroads. I can't decide if this abandonment is a satisfactory destiny for such a fine natural product or whether my use of them as kindling is better. Either way the small, fine wood returns to the Earth from whence it came.

My camera and tripod are in the back seat, but today seems a day just to just absorb the late winter prairie with only my senses. There's a deep canyon off to my left as I approach the wide Yellowstone Valley and I realize it must be Canyon Creek. As I drop down through the ranchettes, the sprawl, the new subdivisions, the urban ooze, I carry back the innocence and peace of the open land with me. It's what I came out for. Thank you, God.

MINDLESS MAN

THE BIG THUNDERHEADS boil up into the high remaining sunlight of this early summer evening—brilliant white and constantly evolving against the blue sky.

The wild lands below, those not yet trammeled by four-wheelers or industrial prospectors, seem to languorously stretch and flex, the flora and fauna part of a complex process that has been evolving and perfecting itself for thousands of years. The smell of sage, pine, and drying grasses has also been refined through eons of seasons. This wild prairie is extremely vulnerable, especially to the rapacious biped who rules the Earth, mindlessly destroying all that is natural in a self-serving, greedy drive to dominance, to power, and to lucre in its many forms.

Although part of the complexity of natural living systems, man neither understands their fragile nature nor the incredible damage his unknowing, uncaring actions inflict. We have reached a point in our world where we use words like "protected" and "sanctuary" and "wildlands" to talk of that tiny bit of the still-natural left. It is insulting to have to use such words because, inherent in their use, is an admission of the havoc we do and have done to our beautiful Earth. We now have to protect what should not need protecting—and, in ultimate irony, to do so from ourselves. But the forces working to take it all are enormously powerful, and those of us concerned are few and weak.

One wonders what will happen when the wild places are gone into the maw of the masticating cancer of mindless man. We have wilderness in our blood; we came from these wild places, and, once we destroy them, we will know subtly in our psyche such places no longer exist. Even if we never visited nor even planned to visit such wildernesses, the realization that we have finally destroyed it all will lessen us as a species. Once wild lands are gone, we cannot return to the peace, nourishment, and revitalization such places provide when—and if—the realization occurs that for the biped to survive, there has to be someplace for us to come back to when the final reckoning occurs.

Our vast cities will become malignant spores like those reflected in the cities of the undead in current media fascination. The remaining waters will be void of life; the remaining wildlife but carrion feeders; the land but weeds and dust that perpetuate the toxicity of our ignorance.

Montana

I envy the wind its freedom
to savor and caress
this sun-blessed land.

I wish I could trace the contours
of the hills as God with creation
must have done.

To run my hands
over the high horizons,
trail my fingers through
the thick velour of grass,
gently follow the swales
of narrow, wandering valleys and
caress the green canopy of trees
like the head of a loved one.

No matter where I wander
Montana travels with me
an intimate companion
who loans me to other places
with gentle bonds of love.

NIGHT NEAR THE ROSEBUD

THERE IS A large, dark cloud over me, hiding the late day's sun. It is the size of future battleship machines of the intergalactic wars—covering half the sky. The West Rosebud Creek murmurs a quarter mile below my sky-storied rest.

The late June light creates masterpieces on the slope of the Beartooth Front—green and dark with the white of small remaining snowbanks dotting high, rocky crags.

I apologize to the sagebrush I've damaged as I drive in for the night. I hope they hear me, as I don't want some sort of nature rebellion occurring in my sleeping bag about three in the dark.

The sun is above and behind the huge war machine, its light creating silver rays like lasers piercing weaknesses in the surrounding clouds and punting east to the coming darkness. The nearby pines to my left start a low hymn with the new wind of evening. I can feel my coyote brothers watching me, sensing. I hope I pass muster—knowing I never can.

There will be no dinner tonight; the six-pack of Blue Boar Ale will have to do, and now that's gone, too.

So eager to get out of town, I also forgot to grab a jacket and borrowed one from my Columbus office. Fueled like Hayduke with the beer, I had driven all the way to Emerald Lake, traveling back over the years since the last time I had been there—sometime before married, before wiser. I had forgotten the incredible beauty of the lily pad lake alongside the road, the bowl of high mountains like a mirrored reflection of a bottomless mirage. I had taken pictures just to remind myself of its beauty and to fill the background of my journal—already full of pictures, clippings, photographs—anything but the writing that's supposed to be there.

It's fifty degrees when I now climb into the back of my Toyota and the old Army arctic sleeping bag. A red sunset feathers all the now-small clouds spreading east—even the gentle virga falling in the distance east across ancient buffalo prairies. A nighthawk soars and booms, alive in its own enjoyment of the huge expanse of sky and evening. Blackbirds down an endless barbed wire fence line sing, "prescillaner, prescillaner." The song is unique and maybe saved in blackbird minds for times like this.

During the late hours of the night, the stillness is so pervasive I catch myself holding my breath, listening to the silence against which my subconscious works. I am curious about morning here on this expensive piece of real estate where I won't trespass again. It comes at five-thirty, fifty-five degrees from north per my compass, the sun angling quickly skyward in this near-solstice time. Both the smell and the light are clean and clear as a newborn day should be.

PRAIRIE DOGS
AND ARROW POINTS

DAWN LIES ACROSS the eastern sky like the side of co-lossal gray fish, its sides blotched clouds against a lightening horizon. I park my car just outside the sign on the gate that says the whole area is closed to any recreation whatsoever. The prairie dogs are up, however, and as far as I could see recreating, despite the danger—me—coming into their new neighborhood.

I am glad to see them here, making use of the abused range. I know the state Land Board would just obliterate them if it felt like it, being God and all, and it being public land, but, for old hard-timers like me, there's pure enjoyment at their audacious industry.

They're one of the cute animals, little pot tummies that slump like beer bellies when they sit up, drag the ground as they run, or just plump out when relaxing on their small mounds. The latter are minor engineering works. As I walk through dog town, the closest critters go underground as I approach while the distant ones take up the sharp yipping that shakes their whole bodies and causes their black-tipped tails to jerk with each yelp.

I had read somewhere that the biggest mounds are sometimes where their drinking water is, and as I stroll the neighborhood, I examine the mounded holes. It looks as if the large mounds have been built by reinforcing the walls of the entry with wet mud pushed and carefully packed in place, their noses leaving many small indentations on the walls. Some of these masterpieces have collapsed, and the chunks have been pushed out of the holes. Some of the fallen dirt clods are as big as the little dogs and easily outweigh them.

I would have liked to have seen this construction in action, but I knew I wouldn't, as spooky as the little dogs have to be to survive. I do muse about getting a ghillie suit and quietly sneaking up to an active mound during the dark hours and being close in first thing in the morning when the sod poodles, as some of the early settlers called them, first come out. They would probably have a heart attack, just seeing something new in their small world. I will probably settle, sometime, for a hidden spot in the nearby sagebrush and my spotting scope.

Their villages dot just the open, old bunch grass prairies that the Land Board with its grazing practices has denuded. It provides the little guys good sight distance from each mound, with the outlying holes constituting the frontier like Israeli villages in the disputed territories. The edges of the old growth sagebrush ring the villages, and I sense the danger therein, as coyotes can hide there and wait for such tasty little dinners. But a healthy prairie dog village is connected like all things in nature, reflecting available food for both winged and footed carnivores as well as homes for burrowing owls, salamanders, and snakes. To see the endangered black-footed ferret is too much to expect in such an increasingly managed wildlife manifest.

I kick an old cow pie, a habit intended to spread its fertilizer wider over a hungry land. The prairie undulates, winter-gray sagebrush hiding coulees and broad swales, where at times looking up from my constant ground watching, I find myself alone, a silent, timeless world of sky and prairie in all directions. I come up on weathered sandstone that seems to have bubbled up from the Earth in rounded layers. I know the opposite actually happened, that the earth has weathered away the sandstone, sculpting it silently in hoodoos.

This area is far enough from city traffic to have no new graffiti, and what is here is older than me, probably dating back to the homestead dreams of the early 19th century. I walk around the sleeping stones trying to figure how to capture their beauty and essence in an imaginary photograph—and failing. Perhaps some things are just meant to be seen and not depicted in two dimensions. Hawks have marked the tops of the stone above my head, and the endless wind has carved away the base. From a distance, the mounds look small, but coming into them, the land drops away and the sculpture stands dignified and tall.

I climb the outcropping to better view the many cracks and small crevasses on the face of the stone, later feeling guilty about the abuse I must have done to the delicate lichen, which can take fifty years to reach the size of a quarter. The latter seems alive, a green and yellow covering of hard velvet still wet from the light rain that had fallen during the night; the colors, without the harsh sunlight to fade them, vibrate. The stones strike me as being almost alive, and perhaps they are, patiently waiting through time for the realization of such things by supposedly more sentient beings.

The day has become almost painfully bright with the spring sun behind the low-moisture clouds, and I keep my eyes moving across the life at my feet. Open areas between the sage are often littered with rocks of various colors and sizes. A beautiful flat pebble gleams jade-like and ends up in my pocket. I wonder where they come from, how they have been so polished and smooth; they beg to be touched and rubbed. I put them in plates of water around my potted house plants, each reminding me of these pleasant sojourns across this precious land. Two small chips of obsidian eventually also accumulate in my pocket, pack-rat-like. The black glass rock had been worked hundreds of years ago by nomads moving through or stopping here. I wonder at their provenance but can only guess, trying to discern ancient history by a delicate, still undeveloped, sense of psychic feel.

A small pile of old garbage rendered benign by the endless corrosion of the elements offends the ground in front of me. Pottery from colorful plates, gum-colored ceramic from an old crock, glassware turning purple from many suns, and rusted bits of tin almost entirely gone. I pick up the pretty purple glass splinter tinted with time—the bottom of a drinking glass. It too joined the pack-rat pocket, maybe to hang on a long string endlessly turning in the sunlight of a south-facing window, spreading its secret history joyfully on the walls of my life.

The wind carries the sound of neighborhood dogs from the latest bit of sprawl soon to swallow these gentle swales. I keep my hands in my coat as the weather turns colder in the maturing day. Looking up and to the west, the horizon is gone in a moving gray cloud of rain or snow. I'm thinking snow because of how cold it has gotten, wishing once again I had brought rain gear and, maybe, a compass and thermometer. I always seem to bring along too much stuff on these soothing walks, so this time I have nothing but a light coat and my field glasses hanging around my neck under my coat zipper. The trail I have been following turns north, and I realize I could have walked to the destination rocks directly.

Leaving the beautiful, chapel-like stones, I'm glad I have been heading into the wind all morning. Now I start back for my car, the wind and the approaching squall behind me. Soon the snow comes earnestly, pushed by the wind, and flying away in front of me like I am moving backward in a Star Wars preamble.

WHEN THE SKUNKBRUSH TURNS

Pulling up the hood of my sweatshirt and my windbreaker brings the silent world even closer, and I revel in the storm swirling around me, covering my windward side with snow. First, it comes in small flakes, then in hard pebbles that I can catch on my tongue or, for moments, in my palm. I know I'm not dressed for prolonged exposure to this wind, snow, and moisture. I'm glad my car is somewhere ahead of me where I can now hear traffic on Highway 3. I can't see my car. I find it interesting enough—and slightly disturbing—that I tend to circle to the right as I walk in the blinding storm. It takes effort to keep in a straight line, doing so every time I glimpse the horizon through the swirling snow.

The ground is soaking up the moisture, and my boots are getting heavy with gumbo mud as I approach the fence line along the highway. The snow, now in large flake clusters and soaking my coat, is covering my face with the fresh and pure kisses of spring, and I wonder why we don't have more names for it.

SHE-LISH-GA[4]

CROW CHIEF PLENTY Coups, last of the great chiefs, in battle wore the legs and feet of the chickadee braided into the long black hair behind his ear.

After the Crow elders listened to an early vision received by this future chief, they told Plenty Coups, "The chickadee is your medicine. We must be wise like the chickadee." And he honored this tiny bird throughout his life. Power from and communication between species is something most people don't believe in now—or even try and understand.

I think, however, that a lot people wish their pets could speak or wish they could understand what their dog or horse is trying to say. I remember once, back when the Plenty Coups museum was in its more derelict years, I went out a January-bright sunny day to try and meditate on Arrow Creek as the chief had often done. (I had been reading his biography, *American.*) It was one of those sleepy winter days of dry cold and low, eye-watering sun, and the water in the small creek was frozen.

I sat on a spot of dry grass, crossed my legs, and did my best meditation; I wasn't too successful. However, later, as I walked back through the deserted yard of Plenty

---

4 Previously published in *Last Best News*, Billings, Montana, January 27, 2017.

Coups' old house to the parking lot, a chickadee joined me, close over my right shoulder, pacing me as it were from branch to branch, and providing a steady, chattering monologue.

I thought of the old and powerful chief and realized something was communicating with me. It excited me. I felt honored but frustrated that I didn't understand more.

Today, as I walk to the Yellowstone River across Norm's Island, the smell of sugar beet processing drifts in the late winter air, along with a humidity missing in the dry crunch of dead winter. The sun is still low as it was at Plenty Coups Park, but the light is already hours longer than December. The day is quiet with soft background noises of cars crossing Blue Creek Bridge, the squawks of some of Billings' extensive crow population passing over, and, nearby, the slightly burred chirping of chickadees. I smile knowing this small member of the titmice family is never still; when they're not flying, they hop—never walking, and when neither flying or hopping, they're clinging to or hanging upside down from branches with specialized leg muscles.

The Crows, the Absáaloke, call the chickadee *she-lish-ga*. Said to have one of the most complicated social structures of any feeder bird, it also has a large vocabulary of calls—more than fifteen. The distinguishing vocalization *chick-a-dee-dee* is, according to the Cornell Laboratory of Ornithology, one of the most complex vocalizations in the animal kingdom. The male's *fee-bee* call in spring is separated by one complete note (that's more than I learned about music in all of high school and college). Chickadees lay their eggs between mid-April and early July, beginning one to two days after the nest is finished. The female lays one egg per day, in the morning, before coffee; they have one brood per season, and they do not reuse old nest sites.

Like grizzlies, chickadees are omnivorous, but so light you could mail three of them for the price of a first-class stamp. When it falls below ten degrees, they slow their metabolisms and do a form of hibernation. During such weather, chickadees need twenty times more food than in the summer, and their survival rate doubles when they have access to bird feeders. They flock in winter to protect their feeding ground—usually an area of about twenty acres, and the pattern of flocking is a popular subject of many bird researchers and, probably, chaos theorists.

Enough feather trivia. As noted by the Crow elders, the wise chickadee relies on the memory of food caches it made in the warm seasons. Scientists have determined that the hippocampus (the portion of the forebrain crucial for memory formation/storage and spatial learning) of the chickadee is about three times larger than non-food storers.

WHEN THE SKUNKBRUSH TURNS

Most small birds enter kind of a catatonic state when taken by hawks or cats. I recently saw a chickadee grabbed by a sharp-shinned hawk. The frightened—and probably angry—little bird didn't give up; in the talons of the fierce accipiter it screamed all the way up and out of hearing. Strong medicine befitting this special Montana bird—and a great chief.

Sky

I am a student of sky and
wide open buffalo prairies.
The great clouds mix well
the dust and ghostly memories
of vast herds and warriors
who still linger
in the quiet of summer evenings.
The dark underbelly of thunderheads
claims the gray of sagebrush,
and into the scent of night
the shimmering evening melts.
Even the clouds come to earth
on the fine line of faraway horizons,
a path in which the years
and millenniums slip silently by.

TREE TALK

HE PREFERRED TO walk at night, the city streets deserted for television inside the thousand cloned houses. Walking quickly, almost a march at times, to a cadence in his mind, to a jungle path of long ago and those who, dying, left him. Not slow like the old French Legion, but quickly to a tune of "Little Boxes." Funny what you could make a marching song from.

The voices of those dead caught in the trees he spoke to as he passed, especially the tall dark evergreens, a century old and still hearing the war cries of the Absáaloke, tuned always to the essential Earth, screaming silently to soldiers long dead when they're cut down for street improvements or office buildings.

"You are gorgeous, beautiful." Brushing past them, touching them gently with his fingers. The naked ones, too, he encouraged, especially those decimated by powerlines, now just stark structures useful to perching birds.

It helped him keep at one with the world he hoped he was aware of after the long evening of bars and drinking and vacuous barmaids smiling. The old, majestic cottonwoods and poplars continued talking amongst themselves, continuing to be there for him. He liked the rough deep bark and looking up into the tree's sky. The crow nesting there knew as other crows do who will survive the millennium planned. Not us.

Trees

It's really hard to talk to trees.
You compliment one
and the others will crowd
your peripheral vision—
"what about me? and me?"

They beckon you
once you speak to them.
I know their cognition.

It's there, waiting
for my awareness to catch up—
before responding.

Like radar or something,
and the more I look,
the more beauty I see—
the more they offer.

Sometimes you just have to say,
"You're all beautiful."
and hurry on.

Even in the night,
they compete
for compliments.

JOURNEY TO LODGE GRASS

I AWAKE AT eighteen minutes after four. Realizing I have twenty-eight minutes until the alarm goes off, I blink—and it does. It's nice to have a sense of purpose and a place to go, to not let the idleness allow thoughts of her.

I do wonder in what subtle manner I choose the necklace I will wear. I have three of them: a white gold one that she gave me long ago with a pendant she had made for me—and which she subsequently permanently disposed of in cat litter so her husband wouldn't find it, a formae cross on a silver chain with her initials that I had made to replace the white gold one, and a new one of heavy white gold, also in formae style with Katherine's "ILY" on the back.

Most of the stuff is loaded, and I decide not to put on my boots. Arriving on the distant ranch and having to put my boots on while sitting there in the early morning will allow my something to catch up with the trip through the darkness. I was going to put hot tea in the large thermal cup she had left in my car once upon a time, but decided to just brew the one usual cup of green tea, pour it in a non-spill ceramic cup with a rubber plated bottom, and put it on my dash.

Way down the interstate highway and safely into the early morning night, I eat a peanut butter sandwich and sip hot tea, appreciating the essentials of it all.

Comfortable in the night, driving southeast across the ancient buffalo prairies, I realize the sky outside is sparkling with stars and planets, constellations, the whispy blur of the Milky Way, all against the blue-black depth of space. The Big Dipper stands straight up, tiptoeing on its handle. The Saab's dashboard says thirty-one degrees out while we cruise at seventy-six miles per hour quietly through the dark. KEMC classical radio gradually strains the remnants of my dreams away, and new cell towers blink cold, white lights in the air along the interstate highway.

The town of Hardin glows against the dark sky before the hills unfold beside me, a sprawl of community with high billboards and too many advertisements that interrupt the rhythm of my travels. I briefly wish I could have kissed the still sleeping eyes of the one I love before I jerk that softness back to the road in front of me and the highway sign flashing by saying, "Entering the Crow Indian Reservation." The Bighorn River Bridge clicks beneath me. In the distance, three orange-yellow lights move unswervingly toward me, pulling a coal unit-train from the Sarpy Creek Mine, bound for the fires of Billings' powerplants.

WHEN THE SKUNKBRUSH TURNS

A beat-up Ford Bronco driven by a Native American pulls onto the road in front of me. I move over to the passing lane. A flapping, white towel covers his left rear window and un-dimmed headlights glare at the back of my head, as my fellow man invades the night space that has been mine—and with his usual alacrity.

I wind up through what I know is the beautiful low-lying Wolf Mountains before exiting the interstate at the Lodge Grass off-ramp. The darkness hides the disaster that is this place, and I continue on through the asleep community southwest, following earlier directions. To my left now, the sky is dusty pearl with mists of cloud visible along the horizon, a knife edge of black hills undulating south. Leaving the pavement, I continue to higher country but keep the brightening horizon to my left. Paleness in high forms emerges in my view, gradually revealing itself as snow. I have come from the river valley where I live to a higher country already in winter.

I pull around the ranch house in the valley of Lodge Grass Creek looking for my friend's pickup—after finding the hoped-for name on the mailbox. Opening my car door in the cold new light of day, I stretch and put on my boots.

I've come down here to photograph a small cattle round-up on a friend's place. I've been looking for something hopefully creative to do to keep from pining over her and to enjoy what may be another yellow-orange, fall day. The ranch is the last one on Lodge Grass Creek, having been there at least a couple of generations. Looking up the cottonwood-colored valley a short distance to the southwestern horizon, snow covers the hills, and a distant black horizon is Wyoming's Bighorn Mountains. My friend walks out with me in the predawn and orients me. The hills we were looking at lead gradually up and up, dropping off suddenly in a high precipice that immediately attracts me.

I'm introduced to all the wranglers, friends, and family as everyone coffees up. Most of the men will be on ATVs, but one family and a couple young women are opting for the old-fashioned way—horseback. Raised like a slave on a hard-scrabble ranch, I'm not enthralled with either the small roundup or the horses, but realize there is beauty here. The horses of city folk and their paraphernalia and formal exercises are a turnoff, but a sweaty, hard-working little cow pony along with a knowledgeable rider is a whole 'nother story. Being too shy to ask for posed pictures, I try unsuccessfully to capture some of the horses and riders. I think later of those I missed.

I hump my camera and tripod up the cold, snow-spattered hillside just after the whole operation has roared past. The altitude, last night's stingers, and the cold leave me huffing. The bright morning hills are glowing with the sun bumping up over the close horizon, sun and cattle both cresting the hill in front of me at the same time. Not the best place to be for photography, but I try and work with what I have—enjoying all of it. The mostly black Angus, with some white faces among them, stream by, many stopping to ogle me and bawl their concern. Soon the herders and mass of cattle are past, down the hill, and going into the pens by the ranch house. I amble down the hill, put my tripod in the Saab, and spent the rest of the morning watching the men separate this year's calves from their mothers, the heifers from the steers, and the keepers from the rest. All the rest are loaded onto large semi-trailers, driven by truckers who think they're current renditions of old-time cowboys, and quickly hauled into the loading pens at Lodge Grass; from there it's all downhill for the cows.

I'm invited to come to the pens where everyone will eat lunch. I want to hike up into the distant snow and that high point of earlier in the morning, but this is another man's land.

At the pens, I decide to stay and talk with the women instead of standing with the men watching the unloading. There is little activity here. Both my friend's wife and daughter are attractive, vivacious women. Plus, the dogs are here, as is the food and drink and the kids. And I have my camera. The day has matured to clear, warm, and calm, the kind which memories and dreams and Montana longings are made. I had soaped up with sunscreen early this morning, so with that and the fact that it was a late-summer, long-shadowing sun, I ignore my skin doctor's advice and enjoy a hatless afternoon.

I'm sleepy though. A rich, beef stew along with the fattening goodies that go with a good cook's menu. I munch potato chips until it's time for the main course. After all the workers eat, I do. I'm the last to pull out, and, after saying my goodbyes, head back up the creek for the turnoff to Fort Smith. As soon as I'm out of sight of the main road, I pull over and take a leak and a nap.

Driving the backroads of Montana reminds one of how big this state is. There is a particular joy in topping a high rise on the roadway that you've been driving toward for twenty minutes and seeing, as far as you can, nothing but more rolling hills and the dry, musty gold of a prairie waiting for snow. The road snakes onward, the mind wanders. I finally reach the road to Fort. Smith but turn north toward St. Xavier then west again toward the small Reservation town of Pryor.

I pass a brown bloody lump on the highway. Thinking it might be a coyote friend, I stop, turn around, and go back. It is. Teeth pulled back in the final grimace, it lies twisted on the uncaring pavement in an uncaring world of the vehicle chrome that caught it. The driver of the latter should listen. There will be a reckoning.

The small coyote's insides are being picked clean by the hawks, various parts of viscera scattered on the road. I pick up the stringy mess of what's left of the small, wild dog and place it alongside the road where its soul can more peacefully remain for that final, short, sense around.

Lots of animals and birds are killed on the roadways, but I try and remove the coyotes I come across, to touch something larger than myself, a connectedness, and quite simply, a knowing—I wouldn't like the last look at my carcass to be that—flattened across the pavement—instantly forgotten. Maybe I do it because it makes me think about the smaller things in my life that may be as important as those I think bigger.

As always, thoughts of her drift in and out of my mind. I haven't decided if it is better to allow her to do this or try and totally not think of her—as if I had any control at all. I almost plow into some cattle on the road, and I realize I didn't get enough sleep in my nap. The scare of almost getting more beef than I want keeps me awake until Pryor. I stop at the dusty, busy, main corner of the town and purchase a Diet Coke; they can't sell beer here on the reservation. The little service station and store does not have walk-in service, but employees hand out whatever is asked for through a small window; the gas pumps are all pay first.

Dust swirls in the parking lot. A battered pickup careens in and a young man gets out, slurring questions about the rodeo in Lame Deer. Another large young man stays in the cab, his face totally transfixed on something midway between the dashboard and his eyes. A young guy and girl of high school-age talk busily between themselves, oblivious to all but their own aspirations. I see them as of an age, not of Pryor or of this tired area of the Rez, but of young people anywhere from Los Angeles to Beirut. It is their humanness that I appreciate.

I drive the narrow winding road down Pryor Creek, going in the direction of its confluence with the Yellowstone River. The old Crows called this small beautiful waterway Arrow Creek, and Chief Plenty Coups, built his white man's house—as required by the Indian Agent--near it. The creek is an ancient passageway funneling nomads for thousands of years through the gap in the mountains and north down the creek to the big river. Yellowing cottonwoods close in the roadway, and I realize that these colorful giants will soon be cut down and bulldozed away and burned as progress widens the road. Part of the way of things, I guess. I gulp the Coke, holding the coldness in my mouth to make my teeth ache to, in turn, hopefully keep my tired brain awake.

Seems to work. I wind down Blue Creek barely glancing at the home where she used to live. Crossing the Yellowstone and the trail overpass she thinks should be called "Cumin-Across." Oh well. Oh freaking well.

I realize when I get home that there is much day left. I do not want to work or create anything, and so, I know, the alcohol will once again get me through another evening without her.

AND THE RAIN COMES

MY DAY DOESN'T really start until I look outside and see what Montana is offering. Sunshine striking gold on sandstone, staining the snow on far away mountaintops. Or clouds obscuring the clean brightness of the prairie sun and the hues of many colors stretching across the land. And, if the wind is holding to its restless keening, the details of distance pulling the eye across a rich carpet of grasses, river valleys, and winding roadways cropped by close, white clouds of every design, the horizon a hundred miles away.

To get away from the buildings and out from under the tame neighborhood trees to the open and magical abyss of endless prairies is to seek re-creation in land and space, and, like a falcon, to soar with ancient spirits—all those who knew this land and grew within its embrace back to the beginning of time.

Sometimes, on a clear morning as the sun scours away the tailings of night, I have the urge to spit on my palms, rub them together, and raise them to the still cool, rising ball of fire like some old shaman, thanking the Great Spirit once again for this life-providing dwarf star. I know even the steam rising from the backs of the cattle reflects more appreciation and awareness than most of my fellow men exhibit.

When the rain comes in its seasons, it seems to do so hesitantly, like a coyote entering a farmyard at midnight or a virgin approaching her lover. The rich earthy smell comes first with an impudent wind pushing the scent of distant pines, dried grasses, and a faint, mysterious odor of electrical energy—like an old battery or a whiff from a mad scientist's lab. The sky holds quick promise of cosmic release and a grand change of scenery. And the rains come. Fence posts darken, leaves become greener, and crystal droplets sparkle from delicate spider webs and rusting barbed wire. I want to merge into the land and the rain and am jealous of the rolling hills their wet embrace; I'm also envious of he who said of the rain, "I am the poem of the Earth..."

As with the sun, the rain moves in different acts across the land. The low, broad valleys pull the rain clouds close into their more private worlds. On the open prairies, long squall lines move randomly over golden grasses and gray sage and rise against immense blue-black skies. The high promontories of the Pryor Mountains seem to snag the moving storms and the angry cloud banks stir wildly, blinking with lightning and resounding with gut-thumping thunder muffled by distance and ancient spirits. Those cloud lines that do pass can circle back in feral fury.

On long hot summer days, the thunderheads form quickly in dazzling white, mountainous towers ascending to astral heights in the robin's-egg blue expanse of Montana sky. If there is rain in this cosmic theater, it will come fast and hard in big, splattering drops that first bounce the dust and then grow to roaring, translucent walls of water that seize attention with their sheer intensity. Passing quickly, the land is drenched, the streets of the towns run with small rivers, and the mood of the living, from cavorting colts in the fields to truck drivers on the interstate highway, is lifted by a momentary awareness of God's grand palette and the power of his brush strokes.

At night, rain is a child's timeless melody, carried softly into the darkness of her bedroom. It cradles all restless minds in momentary and tenuous peace, holding promise of salvation out to us only in the depths of our sleep. The sounds of raindrops touching the Earth, of small streams being created everywhere, of old leaks reopened—a poetry of sound, a soft litany of peace across the tender land.

PRAIRIE

I AM SURROUNDED by prairie—full of wildflowers and native grasses still found where it's too steep to plow and that form a tough cover over the gentle Earth. The hills rise to the sky and spring clouds seem to kiss the land.

Beneath my feet, the dirt is filled with small gravel full of color, agates and jasper. One can see the hardiness zones for the different, blooming plants, early species first out in the valleys, the later blooming higher up. As I walk, big toads jump in small wetlands between the hills. A frightened blue racer buries its head in its coils; the endless wind softly breathing.

My friend Bec brings me a chair, a half-quart of Bacardi, a cup, and a Coke. I could be in the Bahamas instead of back in the Indian Wars of 1872 with their ghosts still scattered across these gentle mounded hills. One hundred and ninety years ago, the Great White Father decreed the Redman submit, and a millennium of years roared back, to be defeated by sheer numbers, doomed by forces beyond even the magic powers of Sitting Bull.

How could it have been to be a proud Lakota—having earned the right to be here, having been for generations—wanting nothing from the rapacious whites but to be left alone? What would have happened if they'd had a Lincoln or a Lee to speak for them instead of only the lance and shield that had served them so well for hundreds of years?

These events remind me of my daughter. The only time I ever spanked her, she backed away from me and granted that she would do as I wanted, but not because it was right. Sheer force persuaded her. As did the U.S. Cavalry against Crazy Horse and Sitting Bull. Right had nothing to do with it.

Sioux men, women, and children died here in these hills; manifest destiny ruled the day—and the Manitou wept.

PRYORS WHY

I ASKED THE oncology nurse what was in the powerful cancer drug being given to my mother. She said the primary component of the drug came from a tree. My gratitude for that particular tree and its pain-relieving ingredient splayed against the irony that they were discovered before mankind had managed to destroy them.

All the meticulous research in the world will never determine the number of miraculous plants, insects, and even animals that have disappeared from the Earth since the advent of man—the anthropocene. And the extermination continues today at an accelerated rate. Over a quarter of all drugs issued by pharmacies still contain components taken from plants.

The natural things that are destroyed or that disappear aren't just in some distant island ecosystem or misty rain forest. Destruction of habitat and alteration of valuable ecosystems occurs at an increasing pace right here in The Last Best Place. I'm referring to improper land use—development of prime agricultural lands, damming of rivers, and pesticide pollution, etc. But, as with most negative reflections of ourselves, the perpetrators tend to be a small minority—whether it's crime in Billings, wildlife poaching, or the destruction of the ancient habitat of the Pryor Mountains.

Perhaps people don't know the value of such a place as the Pryors, and, not knowing, don't care. Most people tend to care about what they know about.

The Pryor Mountains are a unique island in the great sea of Montana—greatly sensitive to and affected by man because of their proximity to the largest urban area in the state. Even having to go through Bridger, as the direct, Pryor Gap route is presently fenced off, the mountains are only an hour away.

The area's complexities begin almost immediately after leaving the paving of US Highway 310. The land is dry, much of it BLM, and yet this is where a state fish hatchery is located, artesian springs gush to the surface, and huge irrigation sprinklers shower tons of water on the arid land. The poorly constructed road across Crow Reservation land sometimes is nearly impassable due to the ruts larger vehicles have gouged The latter improves to relatively smoothness with proper width, composition, and drainage as soon as one enters the National Forest, one of three federal agencies that provide a disjointed administration for the Pryors. Soon the flat land narrows to the Valley of Sage Creek and the small mountains themselves rise on either side. Looking back, you find you have been swallowed by the mountains and are now within a magic place.

Many long-established all-terrain vehicles (ATV) trails branch off the main road. While the federal government tries to determine a transportation policy for the mountains, the five-percenters have plowed new trails to every conceivable place in the belief that it is their God-given right to go anywhere, anytime on their nimble ATVs. The failure of the administrative agencies to police them reflects the failure of man to protect and save this island range.

Even after adopting a transportation plan, the governing agencies do not have the will, manpower, or political leadership to be visible and effective in the many canyons and special areas of the Pryors. Administering this mountain treasure is often just another job to those who are supposed to do so; they get paid the same whether policies succeed or fail. The more contention there is in public meetings, the harder their jobs are and the less inclined they are to listen to those who make the decisions difficult—much less to the silent rhythms of the vulnerable island mountains.Why is it so onerous and necessary for people who care to have to fight to protect a place of caves that contain the animal history of Montana back thousands of years? One cave so marvelous that the giant, prehistoric bear that fell into its depths left huge claw marks in the side of the wall that can still be seen, its bones now mixed with the prehistoric native camels and the miniature horses on the floor. This cave hasn't even begun to be explored, but it, too, had to be protected from vandals by closing the entrance.

Other caves are of the people who have lived here, to say nothing of the Little People of Native American legend who populated this area in the not so recent past. And it should be noted that because of what is happening to their special place, even the Little People might have left the area.

The three citadel peaks above the Reservation town of Pryor guard the now-fenced entrance to Pryor Gap and an old railroad bed that once reflected another dream of white men. Sacred to Native Americans, these distinctive peaks contain the graves and vision sites of thousands of years of nomads. A trail leading along the west side of the Big Horn Canyon is marked by cairns that were built up over eons of use as a most ancient of trading routes—long before the Spanish and the French ever even visualized such a country.

Like the claw marks of the great bear, the uniquely striped legs of some of the mustangs grazing the wild horse range are another tangible link to an older time.

The Pryors are not just a single mountain ecosystem but a collection of several such, as found in few places in the country. Dropping down out of Crooked Creek Canyon on the southeast side, one crosses the rain shadow caused by East Pryor Mountain, the driest place in Montana. Covered with creosote bushes and green Rocky Mountain junipers in brilliant contrast to a deep-red soil. On top of the several mountain plateaus, ancient juniper dating from the time of Christ survive the harsh winter winds. From the lofty heights with their big sky views of other distant mountain ranges and lowland farming communities, one drops to the dizzying depths of the Big Horn Canyon, dammed now and holding back the sparkling waters in the Yellowtail Reservoir.

Boaters on the lake admire the sheer walls rising on each side of their narrow passageway, realizing when they go ashore that these walls are themselves contained in still a larger valley and the mountains continue upward and beyond to the Dryhead Overlook and Wyoming's Bighorn Mountains.

This island range is not a commodity to be utilized for the sole benefit of man and at his pleasure. They are part of us, part of that large matrix of earth and sky in which mankind is—starting to realize almost too late—invested, and the health of the community of man is inexorably tied to the health of the overall matrix. Man, with all his technology, cannot forge individually ahead without bringing the community from whence he has sprung over the eons along with him. He cannot invent and create fast enough to outrun the fate of himself on the Earth. We need to take care of all things including each other to truly progress.

We here in southcentral Montana do not have the luxury of alibi for wanton exploitation of our natural assets. The Pryor hillsides do not have to be scarred because people are starving and need to till the fragile soil. As one writer noted, how can people who love their children act in such ways detrimental to the world in which their children will live?" If we want to take all that we feel we have a right to currently, what will we leave the generations that follow? There are still places in the Pryors that do not have vehicle tracks on them, but such places are becoming fewer.   What is it worth to a child to walk across the desert on the east side of Pryors and not encounter the tracks of motorcycles and ATVs, to imagine that maybe his small footsteps may be the first on that particular piece of Earth? To be able to get out of the car and wander among the ancient juniper and pick up devil's toenails, small star clusters of vertebrates millions of years old; to sit in the coolness of an ice cave without hearing the distant sounds of motors; to imagine what life was like when the cave and the fire within was all the protection the small group of humans had. It is from these experiences that a child's imagination creates.

The Pryors is that kind of place, a source of visions, a land still warped in time and space that allows us to see ourselves reflected in the flowers and snowfields and the eyes of the mustangs and spooky scat of large mammals. It speaks to us. We need to listen.

There are places here where fine red sand swirls in small deserts around the wind-tuned hoodoos, so clean and smooth the track of a rattlesnake can be discerned like some ghost print on the sun-warmed surface. Places in

Petroglyph Canyon where the unexplainable visions of another people crowd hidden walls, and in the midday shadows of the narrow canyon the voices of the surrounding land seem to echo plaintively like wolf song before the sounds of ATVs can crowd the silence.

This is our heritage and none have the right to scratch the painted walls, leave their lunch wrappers in the clean dry bed of a delicate canyon, or tear the hardy bunch grass of the flat land that conceals this place.

Our children will come here. It is a magic place. And they will notice what we have left them. They will wonder why we couldn't have left at least some places alone— some places outside the tracts of methane wells, the extinct plovers, the contrails of congestion, the pallid scrum of pollution in the valleys' skies, the wheel-scarred hillsides that won't heal in their lifetimes.

They will need places like the Pryors to center them, to reconnect to the Earth, to their past, to who they are, to places away from latest technology's promise. For even technology cannot advance in vacuums of awareness. Creativity needs the timeless sustenance of the past and the natural places of the present. It is from such places that man advances. And when they come here seeking solace and recreation, to encounter the ruts of their fathers filled with the thistles of that time, they will rightfully wonder. And the healing secrets of the trees will have long disappeared.

SUMMER AT WHITEBIRD

COTTONWOOD SEEDS IN their silvery finery float down lazily, kissing ever so lightly the clear Stillwater River. Carried away, I hope, to become more trees emblematic of the Montana prairies and foothills.

My bony old butt is getting sore sitting on a small rock with just enough dry area above the water to keep my good, dress shorts dry. I hate dress-anything when I'm out in the natural world, so I get up and step back to the bank and lose the shorts and the polo. My small nook is secluded from the rest of the boat landing area of Whitebird Fishing Access. The water rushing by is warm, and I hope the trout have cooler holes in which to survive. The sun is still an hour and a half from setting; the air is still, and it's in the nineties.

The vegetation along the stream is lush with willows and cottonwoods. I've given up trying to keep up with the names of all the plants and trees; it might be that I'm too dumb, or alcohol has killed too many brain cells, or there's too much other trivia in my gray matter to keep flora details continually in my memory. I used to sedulously note plants and record them either in my journal, as a good naturalist; or photograph them; or take samples back to my office for mounting and identification. Too much work, plus I couldn't remember them once I was back in the field a season later.

Two young mule deer eat their way up the bank and into the trees across the river. There are no mosquitoes. I sit cross-legged on an old blanket and drink my Black Dog, wishing I could get this relaxation without the beer.

Finally, restless in the heat, I gather up beer bottles and clothes and put on my sandals. I also pull up the random, spotted knapweed I find around me. The infestation is not too bad, and maybe my effort will hold it back for, at least, a season in this small, isolated area of the world. I put the weed in a garbage can and realize that this is also a camp area; I will return.

On my way out, meandering through the trails, I stop and strip chokecherrie berries. Filling my mouth, I get back in my car and onto the newly reconstructed highway to Columbus. From there I take the old route home at forty leisurely miles per hour on cruise control hoping to see sandhill cranes before state Fish and Game opens their hunting season. I have to settle for a flock of wild turkeys, but that works.

The old highway parallels the interstate. Because it lies slightly below the big, newer road, the sounds of traffic are muted, and I can largely ignore all but the damn Harley-one-person-noise-machines. Off to the right about a quarter-mile is the Yellowstone River, Mother of the prairie here and incredibly beautiful as it winds its shining, summer-green waters below the high cliffs of Kober and Young's points west of Park City.

WHEN THE SKUNKBRUSH TURNS

I stop at Tia and Fritzi's, sisters raised in the area, much of it on the small ranch-farm they still live on. Both spent their careers as schoolteachers, and both are still full of energy and life and reflections of this part of the valley. They aren't home, but several cats cautiously greet me; the smallest with a wet nose and skinny body is probably sick. Another, older cat doesn't bother to move from where it's sprawled on a retaining wall.

One of my best still-life photographs was taken here from their corral gate. I leave a note and continue my meanderings down the road.

Looking for wild plums, I spot some of the small yellow and red fruit in bushes by a small, roadside gully and pull over. I'm on at least my fourth Black Dog and the thorns of the plums don't bother me as much as they probably should. I notice later several bleeding scratches, but the sour, slightly grainy plums are worth it, warm from the sun and from the rich valley earth.

Later, I continue to look for more plums, perhaps a little more accessible, but find none and cruise on into Park City. There I call my mum, my daily check-in to see how she's doing and how her day has been. She tells me my sister Debby has bought a new—for her—Toyota and loves it. Good for Deb.

I continue on the old highway from Park City to Laurel, driving through the underpass and appreciating some south-facing slope land that would be great for a solar home. Yeah, if I were a land baron instead of part-time bum. Like Travis McGee advised, I'm taking my retirement in small doses while I can and while still young enough to enjoy it. Can't buy much land that way, but what the hell. What am I going to remember just before I die, the rough taste of sun-kissed wild plums or purchasing some land and all the payments I made. It would be nice if we could only use the Earth for the time we're here, and then give it back to the Indians and the prairie.

I drive by Chis and Jerry's mobile home and see Jerry getting into his truck. Being my friendly, beer-infused self, I pull in next to him. He's chairman of the Laurel Planning Board, and we discuss that on-going effort since I left as its advisor. We go inside so I can say hi to Chris, who's pissed that Jerry brought me into their messy trailer while she's in sweats. She, too, has cats; at least four come to me. One favorite of Chris's is a black and white with luxurious long black hair and slightly slanted blue eyes. It crawls up on the chairback behind me and gently gnaws my head to let me know there are conditions involved here.

Even though I'm full of beer, I stop at the Laurel Locomotive for more, but mainly for the popcorn. Great popcorn I've enjoyed before and after years of city council and planning meetings. The popcorn machine is gone—another link broken. I have half a tap beer ($1.75

per mug) and leave. I try another bar; it also sucks. Get on the interstate this time and speed home to Cricket and Bud, my cat buddies. It has been a pleasant and productive day, and I'm happily tired.

DAMN PACKRAT[5]

STUMBLING AROUND MY kitchen preparing my two long-haired Dachshunds' (Muki [Moo-key] and Spike) breakfast (crunchy dog food, vitamins, medicine, and yogurt), I saw in the corner of my eye that the peaches on the counter top had funny marks on them. My first thought was that my cat Bud had decided to add some citrus to her diet, as I noticed the marks in not just one peach but three.

Each mark was made by two side by side cuts about three-eighths-inch long and each about an eighth-inch wide. This didn't fit either Bud's much smaller teeth or her sharp, fine claws. I examined some plums nearby and found one had been half eaten. Not the cat, not the doxies, and marks too big for mice. It had to be a damn pack rat.

I've known they are around as I've seen their scat in the barn. Once, when I opened a door, there one was sitting on some lumber looking at me with a "what do you want?" attitude. I didn't bother it because it wasn't bothering me in the house.

Unlike my neighbor, I hate to kill anything—anything that is except mosquitoes and biting buffalo flies; the latter are smaller than the normal housefly and black.

---

5   Originally published in *Montana Today*, April 10, 2017.

They tend to flit around exposed skin, and, unless you succeed in killing them, they are relentless. Must be related to the freakin mosquitoes!

If my neighbor found a resident pack rat, he'd lock and load one of his store of firearms and safari the barn.

I did Google the pack rat. It's correctly called a bushy-tailed wood rat (*Neotoma cinerea*) and it's conservation status is a rodent of least concern. Duh. Somewhere it was also noted that rodents make up forty percent of the mammal species. I identified mine by its large, rounded ears, long, bushy tail, and brown fur peppered with black hairs above white undersides and feet. The tail is supposedly squirrel-like but flattened and is used for balance and warmth. Good climbers with sharp claws, the males are about half-again as big as the females, eleven to eighteen inches long as an adult with half of that being tail; they weigh up to one-and-third pounds.

Wikipedia noted they are very territorial. Well, apparently this one—I hope only one—is attempting to expand his territory. Females have one to two litters per year of up to six pups. They don't hibernate, and rattlesnakes, which will eat pack rats, often take up winter residence in the latter's home. When alarmed, it will drum its hind foot, or, when it's bored, just for the hell of it—but slower. Now I'm paranoid. Is that tapping noise I've heard the damn pack rat!

Well I don't need a pack rat in my house and especially not on my kitchen counter; I am not sure what to do. Like I said, I hate killing things, so I procrastinate. I clean up the counter with anti-bacterial wipes guaranteed to kill flu germs, grudgingly toss the nibbled fruit, and try to figure out where the little shit came from. It probably got on my counter by climbing up an adjacent couch, but how'd he get in in the first place? Opening the shelf doors beneath the counter, I see another plum sitting by a hole in the floor where some plumbing comes up. The hole's been gnawed to enlarge it (rodent means "to gnaw" in Latin), but the pack rat still couldn't get the large plum and himself through the hole. A classic case of one's eyes being bigger than one's stomach; the plum probably weighs as much as he does.

Well, now I'm sure of who the culprit is and how he got into my personal space, and I spend the next hour using the flu wipes and kitchen bleach-based spray cleaner to wipe up the whole area. I also jam steel wool tightly around the hole.

About three o'clock the next morning, I hear a grinding sound coming from the kitchen and figure he's still trying to enlarge his entrance hole. If he's working on that steel wool, he's going to have a hell of a dental bill. I go back to sleep. The next morning there is no sign of the little bastard. I think I'm gaining.

WHEN THE SKUNKBRUSH TURNS

The next night, about the same time, I hear an ominous thumping in the direction of the kitchen. I get out of bed as silently as I can; my doxies continue to softly snore. They wouldn't hear a SWAT team breaking down the door, but if a neighborhood dog barks a mile away, they get very upset—as, subsequently, do I.

I crack open the bedroom door and shine a flashlight into the kitchen. There on the floor looking at me is the little smart aleck. He looks at me like, "Yeah? What?" He also looks so damn cute—big dark eyes, whiskers around a twitching nose, and a long distinct tail with a flattened pattern that almost looks like it's been braided dragging behind him on the floor. He turns around to leave and his profile reminds me of a PT Cruiser—small forward with a big butt behind.

I need to deal with this guy; we can't cohabitate. The next day I explore the laundry room to which he had gone last night. Turns out there's an old lint tube that comes up through the floor behind the washer, and it's his personal doorway to all things mine. It gets plugged with steel wool, also. I'm hoping this will be effective enough, so I can avoid more drastic measures.

I don't want to use poison because it spreads into the ecosystem; whatever may eat the rat is also poisoned, ad nauseum. I ask my brother-in-law, a neighboring farmer, how to catch pack rats, and he suggests filling a five-gallon bucket one-quarter full of water and oats and then provide a pathway to the top, like a board or something similar for the pack rat to walk on. He gets to the top, wants the food, falls in, can't get out, and drowns. Voila!

Because my kitchen seems to be his destination, I put my improvised rat killer in the middle of the floor and hope that I don't meet it inadvertently in the middle of a nocturnal pee run. Nothing pisses me off more than my own stupidity.

For the next five nights, my third ear is tuned to the sound of splashing. Never hear it, and I remove the water trap.

I buy a rattrap—a real nefarious looking killing machine. It's just like the old mousetrap that you put a piece of cheese on a trigger that releases a spring-loaded wire that slams down on the head, killing the small victim. Only the rattrap is about ten times larger, like going from a BB gun to a 12-gauge. It looks ominous as hell sitting on my counter, and I definitely don't want to forget it's there; I treat it gingerly like an armed IED, as it'd probably take my arm off if I inadvertently trip it.

Finally, I hear the big bang in the night. I get up. Muki and Spike continue to snore. The trap is empty of the cheese and of the pack rat. How did he do that?! He must know some trick. He can't be that fast! But he's definitely not in attendance.

I keep trying. I catch him eventually and the process, of course, kills him, so it's a Pyrrhic victory for me. They don't come back to my kitchen, but I know they are in the attached garage and it's only a matter of time.

It is, of course, through their ability to produce multiple times and multiple babies that they, as a fed-upon species, survive. But it's the same maternal instinct our mothers had for us that their mothers bestow on their young. We ignore this reality and just treat these small mammals as rodents. For a good example of maternal and familial feelings in rodents, look at the scenario around a road-killed racoon. When one of a family is killed, other members tend to stay with their dead, try and protect them, and probably grieve for them until, more often than not, these big emotions in their small owners are also smashed by the next on-rushing car.

Next, I buy commercial grade, anti-rodent sonar that is supposed to be such a sound irritant to small things that it keeps them away. I put one on the floor in the corner of the kitchen thinking it will cover that area. I put the other on the garage floor outside the back door to try and block that passageway.

Both seem to work for a while, then one morning I again notice rat and mice scat on my counter. I re-read the instructions and note that it operates line of sight only, and anything can block the beam, from the corner of the counter to a water glass.

CAL CUMIN

I know one of the big boy's still in the garage, and kid you not, I think he's trying to work around the sensor there. Mouthful by packrat mouthful, he or she has created a wall of fiberglass insulation around the front of the sensor on the garage floor-- like he's trying to cover it up or block it, and like he understands what it does and is trying to mute the signal. Go figure.

I'm not sure who's going to win this.

SNOW[6]

SNOW. I KNOW when it's coming toward my home at night here on the prairie; the lights farthest away from my picture windows fade slowly one by one until there is only surrounding darkness. If there is no wind, the snow comes in great silence, air and sound seemingly suppressed between the falling snow and the ground.

I turn off the reading lamp behind me to rest my eyes from the exigencies of Jean Lartéguy or James Lee Burke. My doxies are on my lap, oblivious to everything and exactly where they want to be.

The native people of the far north may have hundreds of words for the different kinds and characteristics of snow. These same natives just changed the name of Barrow, Alaska, to Utqiagvik. If that's close to one of their words for snow, I'm glad we further south on the continent have a simpler vocabulary. Although, after weeks on end of cold and snow and wind, I tend to add pejoratives when referring to the white stuff.

Barrow, named after Clyde Barrow, Bonnie Parker's boyfriend (well, maybe not) was a fine old name, but Utqiagvik does have a certain cachet to it.

---

6   Originally published in *Last Best News*, Billings, Montana January 12, 2017.

Even here in this mid-continent swath, we have several kinds of snow. First comes the overcast with large, floating snowflakes of every intricate pattern that stick to branches, guardrails, and everything else they touch, including dogs and horses. This is the snow from the ponderosa that eventually falls on my bare neck as I shovel the walk for my two low-slung buddies. Both my doggies are old now but still have the excited energy to charge gleefully out into the snowy yard, barking their goofy heads off and plowing through the snow on four-inch legs. However, on the way back, in single-digit temperatures, I may have to rescue them.

The next snow often changes into finer, harder flakes that seem to fall faster and are denser on the ground. Sometimes, as the temperature changes rapidly, the snow may suddenly harden into small pebbles that look like de-icer on the bare sidewalk and make noise as they hit the wood deck and windows.

After the snow on the roads is plowed, either by a neighbor with his skidsteer or state or county road crews, and the original art of blanketed snow violated, the prairie wind takes over. Approaching the jagged piles of pushed snow, smoothing the sharp edges and filling the endless small valleys and crevices. Once the snow piles are featureless mounds, the wind gently sculpts long curves and cornices that look like surfer waves frozen in white. This snow is compacted by the wind, good for burrowing snow caves or cutting blocks for snow forts and igloos. I think of these opportunities as I'm forced to cut, block, and lift the three feet of snowbank that has formed on my front sidewalk.

Beyond the now smoothly undulating roadside hills of snow, the wind clears some of the prairie land of snow, piling it up behind sagebrush where cottontails and gray partridges seek shelter. Eventually the sun melts the snow on the south side of prairie plants, so that, looking north, lots of brown and gray bristles of sagebrush can be seen, while looking south, it's still solid snow cover. In the evenings, the setting sun paints all the western edges pink.

During the day, when the sun appears, it adds a frosting of shining crystals to the snow cover, hardening the surface, and slowing some of the drifting. Maybe tomorrow morning the wind will die down.

I've just about run out of pejoratives. It would really be nice is for a chinook, the snow-eater to come.

TWO MOONS

TWO MOON PARK in Billings is named after one of the last Northern Cheyenne chiefs to oppose the white ocean of migration into Montana. Two Moons was the son of Carries-the-Otter, who was killed in Kansas Territory by the 4th U.S. Cavalry in the spring of 1857 in what, according to George Bird Grinnell, was "perhaps the only occasion on which a large body of troops charged Indians with a sabre." I doubt the Indians held that particular perspective in much esteem.

Two Moons, *Ish'i eyo nis'si,* was one of the chiefs leading Cheyenne warriors at the Battle of Greasy Grass, more popularly known as the Battle of the Little Bighorn. Two Moons was also one of the leaders involved in the escape of the Northern Cheyenne from the southern reservation where the U.S. government had placed them.

Two Moons' band was located in the Tongue River-Rosebud area before he surrendered to General Miles after the Battle of Wolf Mountain on January 8, 1877. Two Moons, a chief in his own right of his own band, had been mainly a war chief-military leader, one of many the Cheyennes had—and one of three people named Two Moons living at that time. After he surrendered to Miles and after he developed a favorable relationship with the general, Two Moons gained in stature as a tribal leader. The U.S. government tended to seek out one leader to represent the various Indian tribes, and the U.S. probably gave him much greater importance than he was otherwise provided within the Cheyenne culture. As Cheyenne historian, John Stands-in-Timber noted, "most Cheyenne chiefs were made famous by the white people."

General Miles arranged with Two Moons and his warriors that—if they would stop fighting him—he would hire them to help fight other tribes; provide Two Moons' people with houses, farming tools, and rations; and let them choose the place for their own reservation. By giving up their weapons and horses, again according to John Stands-in-Timber, the Cheyenne for the first time became a captive people. The Army did enlist the Cheyenne warriors who wanted to do so, and it was the Cheyenne who found Chief Joseph's Nez Perce at the Bear's Paw—closing another sad chapter in the history of the West.

CAL CUMIN

THE OLD PLACE

IT ISN'T JUST a house and yard, or an address on the roadside mailbox. It's a place of things related to a life, and a spot on the face of Earth, however small a part thereof.

The trees in the plant-bare, sunburnt yard, planted in younger years, now reflect the tangled dryness of neglect and uncertainty. The rhubarb's gone to seed, its reddish-brown stalks poking the sky and leaning in the constant wind. A cottontail hesitates; maybe he's invisible. A large bull snake moves silently around a scraggly sagebrush.

A decades-old pickup hasn't been started since last he got in, its seat reflecting the cheeks of his ass over the many hours they were together. The old truck would know of his absence in the way such things become sentient in our culture of motors and human minds. Someone new may try and get it started, or maybe it'll just join the rest of the rusting machinery and to hell with it all. The old man had treated the truck well and been good to its spirit.

In the large, well-built, south-facing metal barn, equipment is lined up neatly: two old tractors, a skid-steer, a small backhoe. The machinery's quiet, as if reflecting hard work guided by strong, calloused hands. Now it all rests like powerful iron animals patiently waiting new assignments.

It is in the old frame house, of course, where awareness last occurred. To step through the doorway is to brush the past and feel the spirits of the now-vacant house rush out. Spiders enjoy the twilight of empty rooms with the shades drawn and in the stillness, undisturbed, they weave their homes, their delicate snares, their aerial highways.

A deer mouse skeleton, perfectly articulated and fine enough for a display case, lies on the old carpet next to the wall. Cause of death unknown. A six-pack of Old Milwaukee nearby awaits a thirst that will never come. Dead millers and flies and rodent turds detail the spaces of nocturnal rendezvous, and the exchange of gossip, food locations, and other whispered tales.

The rooms smell of dry mold, the windows closed and locked in August heat. Dust motes float in the shafts of sunlight leaking through the curtained windows. Once white, filigree drapes shower dust when touched. Family pictures congregate on a small desk, spilling over from the wall above; older ones of cowboy years long ago are high on a shadowed hallway. Unopened mail on the table. Various odd pens, pencil stubs, and scraps of paper reflect a time before computers. Lack of interest in the literary buttressed with the lack of books. A stained couch that makes into a bed sits layered with dust, probably now an apartment complex for the smaller members of the prairie food chain.

A caffeine-stained and chipped, heavy white mug inscribed with "Arcade Bar" sits by a dirt-ringed sink, the last coffee embedded in its sides. One wonders if that was it toward the end—coffee. Coffee and cigarettes.

There's a black phone on the wall and I'm tempted to see if there is a ringtone, but that would be to disturb the musty stillness, like intruding on a crime scene. An intricately carved table lamp with a leaded glass shade probably has stories from a long ways away.

It is the windows that disturb. It's as if the eyes of his soul still peer between the curtains to the rolling prairie and farm fields and see what he must have looked at countless times. There is a sense that maybe he can still see it, through my eyes and that connection of all things. The windows are big, almost to the floor, reflecting love for what could be seen out there. It's still there. The love is fading.

Back of the barn sits a small shack with a camper-shell roof. A mid-size RV bakes in the sun. A stack of old tires, dead black against the field, and a stack of wooden pallets, gray and rotting with the passing time.

He had been the only one to stop by when I first moved in a mile away. Curious, I'm sure, but still friendly and welcoming. Spoke some of the area's history, some of his. And when he drove the old pickup away, I'd learned who the people, my neighbors, were really. The strange one who kept his wife and daughter from going anywhere. The one who had insulted him by saying his backhoe was junk; the woman who worked as a barmaid in Shepherd with the small kids whose husband just went away one day. The retired BLM career man, even older than him, who collects rocks.

A life has ended, a spirit hovers a small time, maybe to see if anyone cares. The home, the buildings, the machinery, the bits and pieces of a life dim, fading, more even before the heart of the place, its parts auctioned, finally disappears.

PETROGLYPH CANYON[7]

ONE OF THE fun things about Petroglyph Canyon is trying to find it. If you're not a point A to point B in the quickest time-type of person, you should try to locate it using maps, references, and second-party directions. It's a challenge but rewarding with its still-quiet solitude, vast openness, and poetry of twisted juniper, fine sand, and rock hoodoos.

Most of the land here is state or BLM, and the tracks made by miners and prospectors still exercising their rights under the antiquated 1876 mining law continue to scar much of the area. The BLM is trying to control off-the-main-roads use, but it's a big country with sparse resources for enforcement.

If the kids in the back seat are restless, if the dog's sick, if you have to be back on pavement by five, or if the vast open makes you nervous, the easiest way to reach the canyon is have someone take you who's been there. There are no signs, probably because this historic treasure cannot as yet be protected. The bullet marks and initials of the personally deficient beside many of the petroglyphs are blatant evidence of the latter.

The drive from Billings is about an hour and a half. Head south from the interstate and Laurel up the beau-

---

7   Originally published in *Montana Magazine,*

tiful Clark Fork Valley and southwest through the small towns of Silesia, Rockvale, Fromberg, and Bridger. The Maverik station just outside the border town of Bridger is where most people stock up on munchies, top off their gas, and get their preference of drink before heading on up to the Pryors. (Just about a mile south of Bridger is a Forest Service Access sign that marks the main road into the central part of the Pryor Range.)

For the canyon, however, keep going south into Wyoming. At the top of almost twenty miles of rise, the road levels off and the south side of the Pryors loom out the windshield to your left. Turn toward the uplift at Warren and go right when the paved road splits. From here on, its a dead reckoning kind of jaunt, heading southeast and keeping to the main road. About eight miles from the non-town of Warren at a cattleguard marked by large tractor tires, a narrow trail to the right materializes out of the stark landscape and heads toward a large butte spotted with junipers—not be attempted with the family car.

From the parking area, it's about a half mile to the stretch of multicolored rock formations, small dunes of fine, wind-blown sand, and gnarly junipers that is the northwest entrance to the canyon—and its most beautiful part. The petroglyphs and pictographs are about a half-mile into the canyon, and, when you see one, you'll begin to see a lot of them. If the family tires of the trek and scrambling over the rocks in the creek bottom, you can climb out at various points and hike the flatter land back to your vehicle. Take your camera and water and wear stout hiking shoes. Enjoy.

YOUNG'S POINT ALONG THE YELLOWSTONE RIVER

NOT MANY PEOPLE can look from their home and point to historic locales along the Yellowstone River. Friends of mine bought an existing home nestled along the river just above Park City. Their southern view is dominated by the several hundred foot-high, rocky outcropping of Young's Point.

This area is historically and geologically identified—coming from the west—as the beginning of the broad and fertile valley of the lower Yellowstone River. From the east, the foothills begin that extend west to the Crazy Mountains, the Beartooth Range, and the Yellowstone National Park uplift. BLM archeologist John Taylor noted in a *Billings Gazette* newspaper article that this is what Captain William Clark on the Voyage of Discovery referred to as "The Point of the Mountains."

From here east, the valley is rich, irrigated, cropland coveted by generations of farmers. It is the western edge of the land, twenty-plus miles to the east, that was bought by the Minnesota Land Improvement Company to launch the real estate development that became Billings, now the largest city in Montana. This land acquisition (controlled mostly by board members of the Northern Pacific Railroad) included 60,000 acres and extended west from the holdings of the more unfortunate speculators of the-then existing town of Coulson.

Today the empty site of Coulson sits along the river just upstream from the Interstate 90 bridge at Billings and is one of that city's undeveloped jewels of future park land. Along the Jim Dutcher Trail, the site is adjacent to the old J.E. Corette power plant, a piece of land that would also be an incredible asset to the city's trails and parks system.

From the top of Young's Point at 4,081 feet, one can look northeast along the frontage road to where Alonzo Young opened his trade store, small boat landing, and post office. In 1879, it was known as Young's Point Hotel and Stage Stop, and—with hooded eyes to screen the interstate, the many existing residences, and the railroad—one can visualize the hurried transfer of mounts and the dust from Pony Express riders. It was to here that word was first brought west of the demise of General Custer's command at the Little Bighorn.

Just west of Young's Point is a smaller sandstone promontory and then the long, vertical cliff roughly paralleling the interstate highway. These are known locally as Kober Point and Tilden Point respectively. Many people mistakenly think the east end of Tilden Point is Young's Point. From the top of Tilden Point, the vertical drop of over 450 feet to the waters of the Yellowstone is awesome.

The flat, valley land that starts here is where Captain William Clark's scouts returning downriver first found trees big enough to build canoes. Clark needed the latter to carry an injured man—and the rest of his small party and its supplies—downstream to his rendezvous with Meriwether Lewis. He wrote in his journal on July 19, 1806, "Those trees appeared tolerably sound and will make canoes of 28 feet in length and about 16 or 18 inches deep and from 16 to 24 inches wide. The men with the three available axes set in and worked until dark."

In the dark hours before the light of next morning, half of Clark's horses were stolen by Crow Indians, but that is another story in the rich tapestry of such tales along the Yellowstone.

Tia Kober and Alfreda (Fritzi) Idleman, who have lived all their lives just west of my friends' place, remember a large cottonwood in their yard: it measured thirty-six feet in circumference.

The predawn wind still rustles the cottonwood leaves, sounding like the murmur of the nearby river or the whispering of ghosts. In spring 2017, a lance leaf cottonwood (different from the prairie cottonwood with its round leaves) was cut down in Joliet that was 78 feet tall and 14 feet wide, estimated by the Natural Resources and Conservation Service as from 140 to160 years old. An existing cottonwood located near the original stage station is at least as big. Clark camped here for about five days.

In the 1890s the first section house in the area for the newly constructed line of the Northern Pacific Railroad was built nearby; the remains are now piled awaiting burning on the edge of a local property owner's land. To the north of the railroad tracks (there used to be three), Tom Snidow raised horses for the U.S. Cavalry during the First World War.

In October 1908, the second worst rail disaster in Montana's history occurred at Wimsett Point just to the west. In a blinding snowstorm, the Northern Pacific Flyer from Helena plowed head-on into a slow-moving freight train that was supposed to be on the Park City siding; the telescoped wreckage killed twenty people—most of the bodies so badly mangled personal effects had to be used for identification. A freight train derailed on the tracks under the silent sandstone cliffs in 1959; no one was hurt this time.

Mr. Clarence Tilden built the two-story frame house in the 1880s in which Tia and Alfreda currently live, and it is for him the long, vertical cliff immediately south across the river is named. A rosebush, brought by covered wagon, still blooms in the sisters' yard. Clarence is the one who went to the college at Bozeman and carried back the first sugar beet seeds, the start of this important industry in the broad Yellowstone and Clark Fork valleys.

WHEN THE SKUNKBRUSH TURNS

The 1937 flood that went through downtown Billings also flooded the area below Young's Point. Hailstones, part of the cloudburst that caused the flooding, scoured the hillsides to the north of pine needles. Three months after the storm, young Tia and Alfreda dug out hailstones—well insulated in pine needles and jammed under a nearby concrete bridge—and made ice cream.

This is just a small part of the history of this Yellowstone River area, what we latecomers can obtain or remember. In addition to the footprints of Clark and his men, countless, anonymous others—nomads, warriors, explorers, soldiers, trappers, women, and children—passed through this area. It is like a horn of plenty, funneling history through here where the flat land narrows along the river.

RAMBLINGS

I ALWAYS WONDER why a plot of grass can be found growing in an area out of character with the surrounding grass; maybe it was a buffalo pound or other kind of killing ground, like the cottonwood hanging trees at the mouth of the Musselshell River. What happened here that still affects the lives of the grasses?

I can imagine the shaping of the land in the beginning, the hills, mountains, and streams, but, starting in Paleolithic times, it's the first humans, then the nomads, and all those who followed—before the advent of European—who fascinate me.

I often look at prairie landscapes lying invitingly before me and wish I had the ability to see all that happened here, to see any remaining evidence left on or just below the surface, hidden in the sagebrush and bunch grass. It would be like a shadow, events occurring over millennia, the evidence still here before me, under my feet, awaiting discovery after their long abeyance, awaiting interpretation and application of their unique histories to what we know of this place.

As it is, however, I am limited to a present awareness devoid of the land's full history and containment. The occasional artifact is like a water drop in an ocean—singular, almost insular, and accessible only through some highly specialized ability of touch, sense—and religion.

WHEN THE SKUNKBRUSH TURNS

I felt, one evening, I had maybe been given some slight insight when, petting my old feral cat Bud and running my finger down her soft black tummy between her tiny nipples, she stretched out languidly on my lap—the warmest place she can find regardless of the temperature of the room—and then, looking into my eyes, reached a forepaw up and gently touched my face.

FORT PECK KIND OF NIGHT

IN THE HIGH beams pushing back the night, the black Angus cattle in the roadside range look like raisins on an oatmeal hillside. When, on open range where there are no fences, a black, 2000-pound cow standing in the middle of the dark road tends to focus one's attention.

Doug's van is crammed with three guys, three cases of beer, sailboards, food, and whatever else is needed to make the two nights out on Fort Peck Reservoir agreeable. We had left Billings three hours earlier and stopped in Roundup for groceries (and beer), and over the intervening miles, had watched this mid-September day go to darkness.

The sunset, seen from the rest stop on state Highway 200, promised a clear night to enjoy the heavens. The land spreads out on either side of the highway, uninterrupted by any lights for many miles. I find this comforting. There are still places like this, and in itself, it is a meditation on solitude.

My thoughtful mood is bolstered by the brandy and crème de menthe I'm sipping as the miles and hours slip by. The bucket seat I'm sitting in is comfortable, and my only task is to enjoy the beginning of the weekend and the total lack of responsibility. The fifty or so deer we pass on the wayside seem surprised when we actually slow down, being more used to the wind sweeping funnel that follows those who barrel down the dark highway. Even the gray, ghostlike images of the deer are graceful and innocent. Saturn sits at ten o'clock high, brilliant in the dark prairie sky.

The Hell Creek Campground and boat launch site is brightly lit. Doug wants to put the boat in immediately, even in the dark. We fiddle around for a few minutes to wait for the space station to rise in the west. It does and promptly disappears in the penumbra of the Earth, an effect I had never taken notice of before. The boat is a 25-foot Starcraft, what a layman like me calls a cabin cruiser. It's an older model, made of aluminum, big and sturdy.

With Doug and the boat in the water, Bruce and I drive away to find a camping spot. In a large open area, Bruce sets up his tent and I opt for the open. Turn on one side during the night and the dark of the huge lake rests under the stars. Turn the other way and be blinded by the lights of marina. Even with the lights, the Milky Way sprawls across the sky; all the familiar constellations of the city night are lost in the brilliance of galaxies above us. An occasional gull squawks, but otherwise it is nicely quiet.

A party in one of the trailer house units is far enough away to be muffled by the darkness. Sleeping lightly, I raise my head occasionally, hoping to see a skunk or fox foraging through the campsite. Throughout the night, coyotes yelp and howl, living up to their Crow Indian name of Song Dog. Once during a particularly long preamble, I thought it might be a wolf calling, but shortly the happy barking of the little coyotes commenced. There are probably wolves in the surrounding Charles M. Russell Wildlife Refuge—I hope so—but they are silent tonight.

In the morning, my stuff is covered with dew, but it quickly dries in the early sunlight—all but the sleeping bag that I later spread in the wind of the speeding boat.

Coffee is the first need, something to quiet the stingers and beer from the night before. Turns out Doug has filled a Thermos, which doesn't seem enough to my dehydrated body, but it works. Bruce and I load our gear and we're off. Doug drives from a captain's chair and Bruce sits beside him in another. I take a small, comfortable bench in the back. Doug speeds at twenty-five miles per hour, and a huge wake follows the heavy boat; it seems we're going fifty. The lake is big, however, and the speed is swallowed in the vastness. The shore is the color of ripe wheat fields; greasewood and pine trees provide what color there is except for the dark soil of the hills.

There is little sandstone here, not like the sharp, steep cliffs we saw in the distance on our way up. The hills are unstable soil mountains that sluff and run with heavy rain. Buttes sculpted by the wind and rain rise on high points in silhouettes like Monument Valley, ancient, eroded ziggurats slowly sinking into the land. Several kinds of gulls float on the water, yelling at each other or maybe just being sociable. Elegant white-throated grebes keep a respectable distance from the boat. The lake level is about twenty feet below its high-water mark, and between the water and the high-water mark, weeds of every kind grow, especially varieties of thistle. This becomes apparent later in the evening when we are searching for a camping spot on-shore, and especially for me in my Tevas.

Our original destination is the UL Bend where the Missouri River used to make a huge horseshoe turn. Bruce said there was an old trail where passengers from the early steamboats would be let off to hoof it over the tongue of land to other side. I wasn't sure why, but it sounded interesting enough to pursue. Near a marina close to our destination, however, we encountered large stumps in the water that were mature cottonwoods back when the lake was first flooded in the late 1930s. The depth gage was reading 43 feet, and the stumps were above water! There were also no navigation lights indicating this hazard. They had to be like rock, tempered by being under water all the intervening years. I imagined not knowing about them and cruising along here at night. Being several hundred feet from shore, one would assume one and one's boat were fairly safe. I noticed thereafter that Doug kept his GPS on the original meander line in the center of the river, regardless of how everything looked from the surface.

At the Devils Creek Campsite, we got off to relieve ourselves and stretch, walking up the hill about a quarter mile to the latrine. Coming back down, we noticed our trusty craft had managed to slip its rope and was gaily drifting away in the steady Fort Peck wind. We were saved by a retired USDA employee from Hardin who had just motored up in his camouflaged skiff. Camo hat and camo shorts and shirt, and wearing insectile dark glasses, the darkly tanned man looked like an Army Ranger. He turned out to be nice as can be, friendly and talkative. He took Doug out to the cruiser and saved our butts. We decided maybe not to go to the UL Bend and seek a place for the night instead.

I'm just sitting in the back, thoroughly enjoying the ride, with nothing to do but look, feel the wind, admire the dirt hills, and drink light beer and clamato juice. It doesn't get much better unless, of course, she's along.

Searching for a good campsite, we pull into a small bay. We set the boat's anchor on the dirt shore and decide to have supper. Because Doug hasn't caught anything in his attempt at bottom fishing, we have spicy hot chili over shredded cheese and chips, Bruce style. It is, of course, delicious except for little black Buffalo flies that like to bite. I fashion a flyswatter from two empty chip bags wrapped around a large brown feather Bruce had found, and try to make a dent in the fly population. There is some satisfaction in just killing the little bastards.

WHEN THE SKUNKBRUSH TURNS

As with the hills, most of the shoreline is mud, with some bentonite, that lovely, fine-grained material used for sealing ponds and drill holes. Getting muddy was a given. Trying to get the bentonitic mud off was something else. Walking in wet Tevas has never been my favorite thing. Walking in wet Tevas with bentonite between one's sole and the sandal is something else again. Add the thistle fields we have to navigate, and the whole thing is a bitch. Bruce and I climb a dirt ridge bereft of any vegetation and about 100-feet high that gives us a spectacular view of the bay where we anchored as well as the vast expanse of lake on the other side—a view that extends for miles in three directions, including that of the coming sunset and space shuttle. I opt to camp up here and Bruce concurs. So, for our hike of the day, we carry all our gear, including coolers, across the thistle fields and up the steep unstable slope, the movable soil ankle deep in places.

The top is worth it. The multihued sunset eclipses the undulating shoreline to the west of us, setting off the darkening land from the glassy surface of the lake. The high dirt buttes jab into the bright horizon of the setting sun. About 8:45 in the still, clear evening we watch the space station go again over again, almost overhead. We just observe the huge display of land, lake, and stars all around us for a while. My old Bushnell seven-power binoculars have good light-gathering ability and provide us with close-ups of the dark areas. Saturn to the south of us reflects on the water like a small moon, while the Milky Way rises from the southern horizon like a celestial fumerole, so bright it also reflects off the small bay where the boat is sitting. We drink the last of the stingers, and, in the quiet beauty of the hot evening, we climb inside our tents for bed. Inside mine, Saturn glows through the wall.

Then comes midnight, three hours into the night, and the gale of an on-coming storm front. From directly overhead, heat lighting explodes the darkness like a world size camera flash-over. The water, which we can't see, sounds like it's boiling. The structure of the ridge we are on seems to funnel the wind up at us from all sides. I lie on my back, and with one hand on each side of the tent, try to keep it from being crushed; even my feet get involved. The force of wind against the thin nylon fabric is like pushing against someone's shoulder. Finally, at four, I wonder why I am working so hard to keep my tent up in the unrelenting wind. I open my door flap, which I had closed to try and reduce the in-flation-deflation patter of the wind attack, and pull loose the fiberglass stays, collapsing the tent on myself and my gear. Then it begins to rain. The latter, however, is light, and I figure I can survive it, especially because we are headed home later in the day—especially if I can get some sleep. Bruce drops his tent soon afterward.

Later in the morning, Doug comes and gets us up, saying we need to be underway. Another front is coming.

CONFLUENCE

AS A WALKER of Montana prairies, my eyes constantly search the ground for arrowheads, shards, gizzard stones, old bullet casings, and similar lost or abandoned minutia of the past. It's early spring, and this area of confluence of what is now called Five Mile Creek with the Yellowstone River is mostly clear of snow. It is still a time of long shadows, the north-facing slopes of the small valley are dark and cold.

But the low-lying sun is achingly brilliant, and the water in the stream sparkles in late-winter glee. The Russian olives have tiny cream-colored buds, but most of the other woody shrubs still wear a dark, almost velvet-like, gray. River gravel is everywhere, from the teepee rings in the winter-gold grasses on the hillside to the washed, colorful pebbles in the oxbows of the creek.

My friend David is an avocational archeologist specializing in the frontier period of Montana, especially that involving the U.S. Cavalry. A father, husband, Billings school teacher, historian, martial artist, and National Guard soldier, he is the prime mover behind the exploration and thorough analysis of the little-known Baker Battlefield on the river just downstream. He's invited me along to explore this area with a metal detector, the best method for finding the artifacts of the period in which he is most interested.

This small and beautiful valley opening to the river is soon to be a public river access and recreation area called John H. Dover Memorial Park for its earliest settler. It is also an area planned to be part of the new bridge across the Yellowstone, connecting to the northern outer belt loop arterial roadway system for Billings. Many people for generations to come will use this area to picnic, walk, launch their canoes, explore the river, and discard their trash.

The site has no known historical importance when compared to the many nearby areas with existing rock art, known battlefields, old forts, etc. Accordingly, the history of this site with its invisible shadows of all that ever happened here will be obscured with only vague references remaining to suggest the richness of its accumulated history. It is not important history. It is just part of the mosaic of heritage we who live and visit here automatically acquire. If we value it, the land lives within us. If we don't, it becomes a place to be used for our passing pleasures and needs.

As a creek bottom, this is a natural place of protection—both from the elements and, historically, from those one may have wished to hide from or to travel unmolested by. It is a passageway through the steep bluffs along the north side of the river, especially when winter ice froze the Yellowstone—before upstream industries and sewage treatment plants warmed the river year-around. It contains a large flat area that makes for a natural campsite. The Old Military Road that once paralleled the Yellowstone also crossed the river here; only a faint wagon rut on a nearby hillside remains.

I found a large hide scraper on that hill—made from quartz river rock. Fitting my hand to the carefully chipped design of the scraper, I felt a tingle of contact with the one who made and used it long ago. The one who, after hefting it or maybe using it to scrape the fat from a large buffalo skin, decided it was not good enough to keep and left it there where it had been created and used. When I have picked up such artifacts in the past from that first one of my boyhood, I always sense for a fleeting moment that—if only I were sensitive enough—I could glean much more from that first, almost electric, contact.

One can explore a site intuitively, observing quietly through half-closed eyelids and listening to the wind and the voices there. The receptive mind can shudder with shock in such meditation at forlorn and bloody places like Medicine Tail Coulee at the Little Bighorn Battlefield. Here, however, one senses not so much conflict as movement. This was a place of passage, a natural river crossing for those first ones following the receding glaciers to the white man's race westward thousands of years later.

In response to the raucous squawk of his detector, David sets the instrument down, and taking his screwdriver, lifts a couple of inches of soil. In the sunny areas around the chokecherry, greasewood, and wild plum, the ground is soft and the digging easy. In the barren areas, however, everything below a half inch is cold, flecked with frozen moisture crystals, and sinewy and tough as old tar. I have an iron stake with a chiseled point, and I use a river rock to pound it into the hard ground. By the end of the day, my keyboard-soft hands will have curled unnaturally into claw-like appendages that will ache for days and the skin will peel where calluses would otherwise form.

Nothing appears in the small hole, and David crumbles the soil directly onto the face of the detector plate, finally getting a response. A small shell casing, dark greenish-brown and flattened on one end, appears once again in the light of day. David identifies it as a .44 Rimfire.

It was a common pistol cartridge, and my imagination jumps to the 1870s, the cowboy era, and the great cattle drives to Montana. I imagine a smallish-built cowhand standing beside his cow pony plinking at a whiskey bottle with his six-shooter or maybe shooting a large prairie rattler. His horse, his bedroll, and his pistol are most of what he owns—the stuff of legends to come. Maybe he's thinking of the girls back at the Crazy Horse Saloon in Miles City, the wild town where he'd collected his drover's pay and left the large herd of longhorns he'd helped drive from Texas.

On the natural campsite area, we have the best luck. It's like whole timeframes of activity occurred here just waiting to be interpreted, explored, and integrated into the known history of the land. A complete pistol bullet tumbled out of one handful of soil. It could have been dropped in the excitement of an attack, fallen from a careless pocket, ejected from the gunbelt of someone trying to stay on a bucking horse, frisky after a cold winter's night. It also dates from the days of Montana's open range and the great trail herds. It is a center-fire bullet, .44 caliber.

David screens the soil from another sounding: it is a metal button from a military uniform with the design of an eagle and shield in the center. David estimates it's probably post-Civil War, and it clearly makes his day. The cavalryman was probably part of one of the Army units from Fort Abraham Lincoln in the Dakota Territory or Fort Ellis near Bozeman, escorting survey crews for the railroad along the Yellowstone, part of the great mix of soldiers, railroaders, homesteaders, fur traders, explorers, bullwhackers, and adventurers in that short and unique milieu on the High Plains, eventually culminating in the sad confrontation at the Little Big-horn in 1876.

A .50/70 caliber shell casing calls us to another nearby spot as does a .45/75, both common rifle shells used in the last half of the nineteenth century. The rifles, built in quantity for military use, were widely obtained and used by Native Americans and civilians outside the military. A .44 Henry shell surfaces, from a weapon used almost exclusively in this area by local tribes.

Toward the end of the day and somehow defining all that has been going on in my imagination, we find a musket ball. It is badly disfigured from encountering heavy bone or rock, but the possibilities immediately intrigue me. Captain Clark took his contingent of the Voyage of Discovery down the Yellowstone just a few hundred feet away in 1807. He and his troops carried flintlock rifles—and used lead musket balls. He notes this creek bottom in his journal where he camped the previous night and as being up-river from Pryor Creek. This damaged ball could have been fired by Captain Clark himself or hunters from his group, ending up on the flat camping area after passing through a fat deer or just ricocheting off sandstone.

Its provenance stays within its rugged exterior. I didn't see it first, or have the opportunity to pick it up after its centuries-long sleep, to feel that peculiarly exhilarating tingle from touching something-someone long ago, something just beyond the cusp of my awareness.

THE RANCH

I THINK I'LL name my place, "The Dead Garden at the Bottom of the Food Chain Ranchette." The latter word refers to the twenty-acre tracts that were carved out of Montana's landscape back in the 1970s before the land subdivision regulations improved. I can see the big sign now—hoisted over the varnished pine logs over the driveway. Can't be any worse an eyesore than the one on Highway 212 that says, "Lotsawatta." That's offensive is several ways.

Here, it's eighteen acres of gumbo and crested wheat grass—and lots of influential weeds. I think this year I've gotten more moisture than in any of the last hundred years, but, even being almost that old, I still wasn't here to keep track. There should be plenty of green around.

I feel the new moniker aptly reflects life here. Unlike some, I haven't tried to make a horse survive on the paltry fare, so it's just me and my two long-haired dachshunds here on the high plains under the Big Sky. In assessing the situation, I realize that the main populace here is those at the very bottom of the local food chain: deer mice, jumping mice, pack rats, voles, gophers, cottontails, and house sparrows. The latter like my bird feeders, but even they go elsewhere to nest and roost. The sparrows spend the day gobbling up my free eats and hopping around my chopped woodpile. There's also a burn pile of branches in the yard that all birds love, and I'm sure there are mice living there also. But the chopped pile? Go figure.

Even starlings only come occasionally, again for the free food. Pretty birds and smart, but I refer to them in other terms for their habit of dropping their loads in flight and spattering everything in their path.

In my years here, I've also seen one frightened elk, Mr. Coyote, antelope in my yard, and one scrawny raccoon the neighbor promptly and proudly shot "right between the eyes" as it looked up at him through the floorboards of his barn. Even the raptors think this is just fly-over country.

The low orders of wildlife are only half of it—nothing grows out here! Nothing I try to grow anyway, no matter how well I prepare the soil and load it with the best fertilizer products from Ace Hardware and plenty of water from my rain collection system. I've even sent away for some specialized fish fertilizer product guaranteed to grow anything anywhere anyhow. Nope. I buy the best product from Gainan's Floral, plant it, nurse it, and coddle the damn things. Nope. Buy special trees designed for these northern climes and guaranteed to grow rapidly, even producing fruit in the first year. Stillborn. I even built up layers of straw and dirt around its scrawny trunk last fall in the forlorn hope of maybe something green happening this spring. Nope.

WHEN THE SKUNKBRUSH TURNS

I planted a plains cottonwood in the road borrow ditch where other same-same trees seem to prosper. I spent last summer carrying gallons of water down to the road, keeping it alive. This spring I searched for signs of life; it had left.

So, I'm learning. I don't have a green thumb; I have a black one. Even my compost piles, carefully layered and prepped as per Facebook videos, turn to dust. A year gone and I can still read the newspaper I dutifully included. I cannot figure that one out at all.

And let's talk hollyhocks, that hardy pioneer of Montana homesteads. I collected seeds of several favorite colors over the year and looked forward to their hardy beauty. The first year, my bed of flowers came up nicely, and the cottontails ate them down to the nubs. The next year, I fenced the flower bed with chicken wire held in place by wooden lathes. I had to rescue one young rabbit from inside the enclosure, but it hadn't done much damage. The hollyhocks grew, but straggly. I carefully separated out the grass growth (crested wheatgrass, of course) and the bindweed. I faithfully watered them and fertilized them with the best I could find. Still scraggly. This year I just let them go, and the bindweed took over.

I tried a raised-bed garden that was doing well until the voles snipped off the roots of everything. I dug the bed out and put down wire mesh and refilled it. That seemed to work last year. Because I'm not planting this season, the weeds are flourishing in it, and I can see a vole tunnel opening in the middle of it, mocking me.

So, this spring's strategy: don't plant anything! The upside of this denial is, however, my reverence and nurturing of anything that does grow here. I'm even tolerant of most weeds. I have a vine in my living room I've had for years, and last fall a seed from a common mallow germinated (yes!) in the large pot. I let it grow. It was dark green, and last winter was definitely a white one outside. Boy, did it grow! Even flowered. Great!

One weed I cannot tolerate is yellow alyssum; a couple of centuries ago it was referred to as "Mad Wort," much more apropos—especially considering its relationship to rabies. It is taking over the rangeland, and the usual lush green of spring in Montana is shaded now with yellow. Some think it's "kinda purty," but wait until this fall when it dries out; the flat seeds stick to everything from shoe laces to dog hair. I'm thinking the forbs will win in the end; even if we manage to nuke ourselves, the weed spores will just rest awhile and then one day push up through the ash and voila!

I inherited trees when I bought this fixer-upper place, ones that had been neglected for years. This was okay for the spruce and ponderosa, but the domestic trees were a tangled mess. Even after I trimmed them up and out, they still look askance at the world. I'm trying to get my Texas buckeye to flourish and still can't believe the former owners planted it here. Native to the warm and humid south, it's stunted but still produces its flowers and amazing fruit. Before fall, it appears leafless and dead.

I am encouraging another natural crop: sunflowers. In the fall, I gather the dried seed heads and carefully plant them where I would like them to appear in the spring. I think the term for that effort again is "fruit-less," literally. I have learned, however, that wherever they grew last year, there will be hundreds of seedlings in the same area in the spring. Eventually, I will have a yard completely full of sunflowers, that is, as long as I don't try and encourage them. Sheesh

One thing I'd really like to see is more alfalfa around my place; I really don't appreciate my field of crested wheatgrass. Currently the alfalfa grows along and in the edges of the roadway pavement, seemingly very hardy. Each fall during my walks I strip handfuls of the dried seeds and scatter them along the trail across my pasture. Absolutely nothing comes of this effort. So last fall, I just threw handfuls of the seed in one or two places so that it was practically layered, sure that it would produce at least some plants. Nope. I even carefully prepared a seedbed after the snow had melted and prior to the spring rains, spreading the seeds gathered last fall and then covering them with a thin layer of dirt. I'm still hoping, but it doesn't look promising. The alyssum is blooming there quite nicely.

BIRDS

I THINK OF myself as a Yellowstone person, not the National Park but the river, the longest undammed river in the lower forty-eight states. It's a sense of being part of this magnificent Montana scape, something ethereal in the blood, blended into genes from an immigrant great-grandfather who was a cavalryman and who, first of my lineage, rooted here. My paternal grandfather came from Canada to the plains of this area, maybe on the run, riding a rustled pinto.

Birds are part of my life, I realize, from the pretty ceramic duck I've had for thirty years, small, fragile, and dropped once, so there's a hole in its side that I am gentle with. The emu from British Columbia where I spent a week with friends beside a cold Canadian river that was milky with glacier parts.

There are the mourning doves that return each year and that I encourage with abundant safflower seeds on my driveway and feeders—whatever it takes including positive thoughts directed to them expressing my appreciation of the delicate form built for speed, and the elegant neck and head, like a Mona Lisa bird. I've managed to keep eight pairs coming back each spring. I say "pairs" but the males are still working on that, ceaselessly pursuing the females. I can't tell if the latter like the chase or eventually capitulate through sheer exhaustion. I chase away the collared doves and their mockery of the mourning dove's mournful call. They weren't even here ten years ago, and now they're driving away the natives. My animosity toward them is shown by simply shooing them away when they come to eat. Like the positive thoughts directed to the mourning doves, the thoughts I send the interlopers are harsh and negative; it seems to work.

There's also the small ceramic sparrow of no particular artistry given to me by a lover long ago. It patiently sits in a kitchen windowsill, unaware that its value lies in the beauty of younger days and will be lost when I'm gone. The live house sparrows outside my windows are my main clients. True to lifelong nature, I like the females best. They are as feisty as their male cohorts, and I find in the uniform gray of their breasts a subtle beauty. Besides, these guys and gals are year-around hardies, often covering my cookie feeder on my porch and, if empty, looking in the window of my office, obviously wondering where their munchies are. Even though I appreciate the house sparrows, it is the smaller tree sparrows I really like. They are feisty, eat the smaller seeds, and strut like blackbirds.

There are also the exotic, South American birds made with brilliant, real feathers. Only about five by seven inches, the hand-carved wood frames and the glass-covered feathers of decades dead birds are unique but are not something I would purchase today. The two pictures were my mother's, and I remember them hanging brightly on her basement wall.

May in this beautiful prairie north of the Yellowstone, and my loggerhead shrikes are back. About three weeks ago a single showed up flashing black and white in his or her swift flight. For a while, I felt sorry for its solitude, thinking the rest of his flock had not survived the winter. About a week later, I noticed there were others. They have nested here for five years, about two feet from my bedroom window. I first became aware of them one spring when one died in its speedy flight, smacking into one of my picture windows. After determining it was dead, I had the opportunity to examine and identify it: loggerhead with its black eye band and white box on the wings. Later, I also identified a northern shrike. They and their families spend the summers here harassing other birds and hanging the occasional mouse from the thorns of my Russian olive trees.

The meadowlarks come in mid-March. One day the prairie is winter quiet except for distant man-made sounds like car traffic on the nearby Red Neck Highway. The next day the swales and pastures are filled with their several songs. It is refreshing after the too-cold winter, but as the summer months wane, I feel a pang when I detect the plaintive note in the unfulfilled courting songs. Life plays out among all of us.

WHEN THE SKUNKBRUSH TURNS

In the winter, besides the close-in chirping chatter of the incessant sparrows, the sounds of the crow and the raven seem most evident, the latter a guttural call that reflects the very wildness out there with the raptors and coyotes. Above my desk, I've got a Innuit classic graphic of the raven that I picked up in an Anchorage museum. I've added real raven tail feathers to it.

On one wall of my office, propped up by about forty books, is a large print of a stork. It, too, has kept up with me, pushed behind the glass and good frame from another, discarded print, its sheer elegance makes one want to pause and agree.

When I watch the sparrows feeding, I look for subtle differences, but sparrows are constantly mutating. Notwithstanding the ongoing variations of gray and black, I look for more distinct signs. These can include slight size differences or behavior differences, ones that scratch the feeder or the ground with both feet at the same time in a kind of hop. It can also be a subtle, darker strip across the eye or just above it, or clearly articulated differences such as distinct white stripes across the head from front to back. I also appreciate the occasional visitors: white-crowned, chipping, and vesper sparrows; horned larks, goldfinches, and various thrushes.

One that teases my attention with its sometime visits is the Say's phoebe. One indolent summer afternoon I heard its unique, short whistle, grabbed the binoculars and tried to carefully note is character. Then to *A Guide to Field Identification, Birds of North America.* (I'm on my third copy and not always from severe reference use— the second one got accidently bathed in the sweetness of brandy and crème de menthe). Back to the binocs. I can never interpret the sonogram that boldly accompanies each bird in this great tome, but, after tentative identification, I checked Google and matched the song.

Sometimes during the summer, I have the privilege of being visited for a week or so by a sage thrasher. A member of the same family as robins, the thrasher is as tall as a robin but slimmer and has a cocky saunter with its long legs.

After daily feasting here, the various species scatter, many flying down to cottonwood homes along the borrow ditch by the paved road. The shrikes do nest here and a starling who has figured out how to get into the flashing of my garage eves. In the winter, the lack of leaves on the cottonwoods expose variously designed nests. Some are sack-like "suspended cup nests," and there are a lot of small bowl nests. A particular beauty I found last fall lying on the road was one of the bowl-like structure made entirely of horse hair; that must have taken some time. It sits now on my bookshelf.

I find the various blackbirds hard to identify, probably an issue of old age eyesight and a brain too small to hold all the things I try to stuff in it. Sometimes I wonder—

when I'm trying to memorize something new (like bird IDs)—what in my brain is being pushed out to make room for this new item. I may need to concentrate on either plants or birds, maybe give up on my attempt to draw every forb on the place in what has been a vain attempt to know my weeds. Maybe it's just a case of CRS.

Anyway, blackbirds aren't very class conscious, that I can tell. A flock of the same on my driveway feed mill often contains red-wing and Brewer blackbirds, starlings, and cowbirds. Sometimes, just watching them is informative. Seems like the cowbird, for instance, has either its head or its tail as high in the air as it can get it, kinda like they're prancing and preening or, on the other hand, looking for satellites. Could be a boy-girl thing, too, as this greening time is prime season for trying to show who's the most handsome or prettiest, has the greatest voice, etc. Regardless of all that show-off stuff, I've noticed that persistence seems to work best—just wear the lady down.

The cowbird is smaller than the others, but that's hard to notice unless the latter are present for comparison. They seem solid black all over until the light hits them good and the brown in the head shows. The cowbird also seems lazy. Besides being all-day gluttons at my feeding sites, they don't build their own nests. They lay their eggs in other, often smaller, birds' nests. When the eggs hatch, the larger cowbird chicks often then push out the smaller chicks of the nest owner-builder, while the cowbird parents return to gluttony at my feeders without any building, maintenance, or even parenting to worry about. These guys also party late. All other birds have headed home, but these guys eat on, heads or butts up. I wonder where they live (and wish they'd go home; this isn't the Salvation Army for cowbirds). I've taken to putting out more safflower seed, as only the mourning doves eat it.

A couple of days ago when I let my two muttskis out at sunrise, two yellow-headed blackbirds were sitting on the wires above me. They did a brief "erk-brrr" greeting and flew off. They did spend the day near but not before I got to add them to my ranchette life list.

Starlings will mix with the various blackbirds. Easy to identify with the white spot-speckled bodies and long beaks. I don't particularly like them as they tend to aerial bomb my outside walls and have figured a way inside my garage to decorate my car for free. But with the paucity, generally, of wildlife around this gumbo desert, I let the starlings be. I enjoy hearing them chatter amongst themselves when I'm inside working with the windows open. Part mockingbird, they do everything from bold whistles to sounding likea herd of cats. I've heard they can be trained like parrots to "talka-da-Englais," and know they're not native to the U.S., having been imported as pets. Talk about needing immigration controls; if they were humans, we'd all be speaking starling.

WHEN THE SKUNKBRUSH TURNS

The Brewers blackbirds are slightly larger than the others, and knowing it—instead of walking—strut around like they own the place. Their shiny black heads are iridescent in the sunlight and their eyes set off by a golden ring.

There is a wall of wooden pallets below me about 400 feet long. I asked my neighbor what it was when I first moved here. He said it was a windbreak. If you can imagine probably a thousand pallets, eight high, you get the idea. I'm the one who needs a windbreak as I'm on top the only rise in the area, but I'm sure it works for whoever lives there. Ugly as sin, but it must be home to thousands of small souls (is there such a thing, or are souls all the same size?)—wood rats, deer mice, cottontails, and whole fraternities of birds, all safe from marauding predators larger than a pallet height. I do imagine the bull snakes cruise this condo area.

The cowbirds have finally picked the cookie-pan feeder outside my office window clean. Now they are apparently working on the fine sand that finds its way into the twenty-pound bags of seed. Kinda reminds me of the old gold assayers in the early mining towns who managed to redeem a regular salary-benefit from each transaction hidden under their long fingernails. I should weigh the sand sometime. Not that it matters much. It's the best wild bird seed mix I can find. I've bought the expensive Niger seed and black oil sunflower seed and mixed and matched, but this Ace Hardware wild bird seed seems to be the most palatable to the surprisingly finicky wild birds.

The cottontail like the corn kernels that the birds toss to the ground.

PRAIRIE THINGS

I WRITE OF Montana prairie birds, read a novel about the Viet Nam carnage, and drink six fingers an evening of Canadian whiskey. Go figure.

When the sunset looks like scrambled eggs on fire in the Japanese panels of my windows, divided by the porch upright; the latter change rapidly, gloriously; flowering crab and alpine glow. The land is olive, fragrant with yellow clover.

Strange, pink cloud rises from its original focus on a distant town, and then up in the air, solitary, blushing.

The land turns black, all absorbing, except for the tinkling lights of distant homes. Above is gray with mixing clouds that continue their journey across the darkening sky as if they had someplace to hurry before darkness overtakes them. They finally disappear into darkness and the galaxies move in.

I love it when the whole landscape is in shadow and, suddenly, the last rays of the sun break through, illuminating in warm golden colors a distant prairie ridge or sandstone cliff. It has happened a hundred million times on this ancient land, and it seems to draw together the spirits of all history still here in its long, bright rays and, for a magic moment, brings them out to play.

Baby cottontails keep tripping my front porch light sensors. I don't think they realize what they are doing—or we're all in trouble.

I love to hear Muki's snore, because I know it means she's content and safe. And, too, because it is basically and unalterably Muki. It reminds me of when I needed to get a urine sample from her for the vet. Finally, as she lowered her bottom half to the ground and I put the large plastic dipper under her, she unknowingly filled it. I felt blessed when I saw the warm, yellow liquid direct from the inside of that little, soft and perfect body. It felt holy, sacred. I almost tasted it.

The rich, thick and deep bunchgrass that covered this old buffalo prairie before the white man came is gone, replaced now with invasive weeds from Europe and Asia. Cheat grass may be the worst due its pervasive resilience. Fully grown out at two feet, it dries into a ferociously energetic tinder, and if, it doesn't burn, each plant produces thousands of seeds for the coming spring. The grasses, like the crested wheatgrass planted with encouragement from the federal government, are almost as bad, becoming unpalatable to cattle and wildlife when dry in late July. In dry evenings, when the lightening comes, the stalking daggers of flame instantly plant rapidly spreading gardens of fire. Fanned by the wind, they race across the night.

Winter Haiku

seen from this hilltop
blowing snow makes a smaller world
Montana winter

the moon is singing
high in the winter-bright sky
coaxing dawn to come

coyote comes to eat
from the snow-covered darkness
roadkill antelope

cold sits on the land
snowstorms from Saskatchewan—
curtain of the night

sandstone bluffs stand
guarding a frozen prairie
February winter

powdery snow blows
in rippling white sheets across
a frozen prairie

CAL CUMIN

watery sunshine—
clear nights of stars and cold
seemingly endless

a cat moves
in the night—quiet as silt
drifting in water

OLD ONE

WELL INTO HIS seventies now, he realized one day that the magnet on the fridge was more accurate than it was a joke he'd thought amusing when he had put it up: "Most of my money I spent on women and whiskey. The rest of it I wasted."

He couldn't say he'd wasted the rest but had never developed any manly interests that carried over into these later years, not even another wife after he'd gotten good riddance of his daughter's mother twenty-five years ago. Now he kind of envied the old couples he sees, if just for the companionship he sensed. He envied, ever so slightly, the great interest other men had in golf or fishing, football, or other sports. He'd tried over his lifetime but had no success. For him, it had been mainly the women, with a little martial arts, flying, reading, history, Montana, animals, and nature in general alongside. What compared, after all, to the intimacies of a beautiful woman, the taste for a form of war, and the freedom of working for oneself—all the things that faded with time and age.

So, he wrote a little and read a lot, realizing the latter was merely filling space, tamping down the ennui, a non-substitute for that which embers still burned deep in his soul.

CAL CUMIN

There was the booze, of course; his stepfather had once been an alcoholic and had told his mother that, if you were going to seriously drink, then drink whiskey. When he realized he was a serious drinker, he did just that, and now consumed about nine ounces of eighty-six-proof Canadian whiskey a day—mixed with water—and maybe preceded by a couple of light beers. He thought he concealed it all pretty well and lived what remained of his life with his two beloved, long-haired dachshunds in a converted trailer house on a dry-land place with great views—and desired nothing more.

EVENING

IT WAS THE best of evenings, coming at the butt end of May in a year of snow and rain. I was enjoying a recently acquired rocking deck chair on my south porch. My closest neighbor is a quarter-mile distant, so his large barking dogs are more of a background than a distraction. The evening is perfectly still, disrupted only by the traffic on the nearby Red Neck Highway and sweetness of scattered birdcalls.

Yellow clover reigns as far as I can see, and its sweet aroma permeates the prairie, a rich mixture of green growing things not yet scalded by the sun.

I am a student of clouds this quiet evening. The snowy clouds of spring still linger, their flat bottoms a moveable ceiling with openings to the translucent blue of space beyond. In the distance, moving regally, billowing thunderheads rise, their whiteness almost blinding, their energy a ferocious beauty, like volcanoes. The tops are ridged like high mountain couloirs and the ribbing remains of old glaciers, resembling jumbled mountain ice fields only softer, like crumbled cheese sprinkles. Longer, flatter clouds scoot by amid wispy popcorn-like puffs—all connected at different elevations by strings of horsetails. Eventually, at least for this Montana day, the giants slowly dissipate in the lengthening evening as twilight approaches. Although, the trunks of the giant thunderheads are still boiling and rising, the high, distant crowns are already sliding down the wind.

A tiny bit of rain fell amidst the prairie wind this evening, not enough to settle even the dust of weeks without. It had a curious quality as it fell and blew through the air above the land. It had gathered some of the heavy forest fire smell. In inhaling the rain, it seemed one also inhaled concentrated smoke. It was unique, sad, and interesting all at the same time. The in-breath was heavier than normal inhalations of rain air or the eye-watering smoke. It was served up in late, dry summer Montana with the media pictures of tall timber burning in some unknown rage.

A piece of rainbow is caught in one cloud, green, yellow, red, and purple, like a soldier's insignia sewn onto the capturing cloud—knowing it must reach terra firma for fulfillment. Beyond the Pryor Mountains far to the south are clouds of another country—Wyoming. For brief seconds, my damaged ears discern a coyote's joyous yip. The evening is complete.

PRAIRIE WINDS ADIEU

IT IS ALWAYS such a unique place to go, even for those who don't love the high Montana plains edged faraway by the glistening Beartooth Mountains.

"We've got volumes of guest books," says Jerry who, with his wife Fran, owns the Prairie Winds Café here in Molt. "They contain names of people from all the United States plus forty-eight countries." Still it's tough to make a go of it, even though in good weather, the Saturday breakfast crowd often had to wait in line outside for a seat, the locals mixing with lots of Billings and Laurel people, a few dogs, and the brightly clad bicyclists.

There's also the ghostly remains of former gas pumps that once stood in front of the old hardware store building. It's all been cleaned up about four times, Jerry says, but the environmental people seem to make a career of it. "They never tell you it's finally clean enough. They just give you a letter saying, "No further action needed at this time," he says. Try and get a bank loan with that kind of certification. In July, another 8,000 cubic feet of soil will be removed.

Jerry says maybe he and Fran will just have an auction in September or sometime, but in the meanwhile, they've got grandkids to visit.

So, on this hot early summer Saturday, those who will miss the Prairie Winds Café the most gather with their lawn chairs, sun umbrellas, cameras, kids, and dogs to express their appreciation of the small café located where the pavement ends on Highway 302. Several of the young girls from area farms who worked as part-time waitresses still seem to exude a clean innocence as they observe the crowd. Lots of pictures are taken, the backdrop of round grain bins, the now dark café, an old grain elevator, and the big open—all vignettes to collective experiences and end of an era.

Proceeds from a breakfast-lunch prepared by the Billings Heights Lions Club will help send the owners off on a badly needed vacation. Not everyone here eats, but at the end of the day, the Lions will have fed 350.

Doug H., a long-time banjo player and member of several local bands, organized the almost-spontaneous event along with two Molt residents. Porta-potties were donated, and the Lions were contacted for providing food. The various bluegrass and country bands that had showed up at the café on Saturday mornings over the eleven years it operated were contacted. The bands had all benefited from the exposure they got at the breakfast soirees playing for the always appreciative audiences.

Nine bands responded and played one after another continually from 8 in the morning to 3:45 in the hot afternoon on an open sound stage pulled into the big lot next to the Molt Community Center. The Unexpected, String Stretchers, Longtime Lonesome Dogs, Spur of the Moment, Southbound, Bluegrass for Breakfast, Song Dog Serenade, Cold Frosty Morning, and Hwy 302— the names of the bands as colorful and memorable as a visit to the small café.

CAL CUMIN

MORNING RIMS WALK

I REALLY GET the feeling of how lucky I am today not to be part of the distant rushing traffic going to work. Instead, I'm on the sandstone rimrocks above the city of Billings on the Black Otter Trail. The still cool sun is four fingers above Emerald Hills, trying still unsuccessfully to burn off the valley mist. White snowbanks of low-lying clouds are still spilling into the valley from the surrounding hills. Fog in the air and heavy dew on the ground.

Clouds of every shape, kind, and altitude seem unable to decide what to agree on and mix with high contrails across Montana's big sky. Smoke and steam rise from valley industries in perfectly straight lines up to a point just higher than these rims before abruptly veering off to the west. Sleek, twin-engine aircraft take off to all compass points from the adjacent airport, some of them only visible when they thrust through the low clouds directly over my head, and I, earthbound, wish I was in the cockpit, eyes on the instruments and the distant horizons. A large, UPS jet thunders into the day.

Although the trail is asphalt, much of the plant life adjacent to it is pure prairie: sedgewort, silver sage, and giant sage near the substation; coneflower, snakeweed, gayfeather; late blooming flax named by Meriwether Lewis; exuberant sunflowers following their namesake; pricklepoppy, wild rose, and yucca; scraggily cotton-

woods and the hardy ponderosa pine where the trail ris-
es. Grasses—native, invader, and ornamentals. Enough
varieties to take back to the busy desk, already cluttered
with arrowheads, books, bones, and photographs, and
work, for a different species every summer day. I still
wouldn't learn them all, having no patience for the va-
garies of botany.

A red tail hawk circles a copse of trees, and two turkey
vultures glide the plaining wind above the rim face.
Shy, peeping, LBB's (little brown birds) that never let
me get close enough to identify them, flit in the grass
and skunkbrush. A flicker attaches itself to the very edge
of the very top of the tallest wooden power pole as if
to claim a sovereignty of sorts, which I'm glad to allow.

It smells of morning with a hint of the coming fall. Back
at my truck, my nose has a drip on the end and my
sandaled toes are cold. My spirit sings.

POWDER RIVER DEPOT

"**NOBODY CARES ABOUT** dead cavalrymen anymore."
I thought of my friend's comment as I headed east from
Billings, Montana, in the early morning dark. A jour-
neyman archeologist, she wanted me to help her inven-
tory and document an old cavalry cantonment at the
confluence of the Powder and Yellowstone rivers—the
"Empty Quarter" as she calls this eastern area of Mon-
tana. Traditional archeology tends to ignore its complex
and colorful frontier history.

As I drive the promise of dawn sinks in the thick fog of
the Hysham Hills. Only the largest objects come out of
the night, ponderosa pines, sandstone cliffs, and the oc-
casional silhouette of a winter-bare cottonwood tree in
isolated beauty. Approaching cars form haloed tunnels
of light quickly moving past.

Slowly the day lightens, but the horizon clouds of morn-
ing claim the quiescent sun. As the fog gradually clears,
a Russell Chatham-like landscape of autumn tree lines,
broad valleys, and spots of black Angus cattle moves out-
ward. Soon the great high plains of Rosebud and then
Prairie County spread to the horizon in all directions.

On a flat sagebrush and cactus-covered land adjacent
to the two rivers, we meet. A steady wind is blowing
from the northeast; the forty degrees seem much colder.
I empathize with the 4,000 infantry and cavalry sent

here early in the spring of 1876 to await dispersion to skirmishes and battles that would mark their place in history. Here at the beginning of summer the Seventh Cavalry stripped to light marching order, drew their rations, and headed west to the Rosebud, the Little Bighorn, and history. They leave at the depot five privates from each company of the Seventh, one non-commissioned officer, and the regimental band.

Flat, rusted cans with leaded seams containing a soldier's diet staple of beans still litter the ground. I wonder, of those Indian fighters who didn't die, desert, or were discharged, how many would have eventually succumbed to lead poisoning. In a small graveyard on a dune-colored bluff overlooking the Yellowstone, sandstone markers show death in mid-life. Further away, the lonely grave of Private William George marks the final stop of a trooper too badly wounded at the Little Bighorn to accompany his fellow injured any further on the steamer *Far West* to Bismarck.

In September 1876, the Yellowstone becomes too low for steamboat travel. The cantonment is abandoned, troops are dispersed to other depots on the Tongue River or Fort Keogh, and General Sheridan's Winter Campaign signals the beginning of the end of the Indian Wars on the northern plains.

A depression near the highway marks the location of a roadhouse that briefly served the soldiers and buffalo hunters, and then, later, was a stage station before the railroad came. The deep tracks of the wagon trails crossing the Powder River still give up shards of whiskey bottles and tableware.

The endless wind must still carry somewhere the shouts of the soldiers, the war cries of the skirmishing Sioux, the whistle of the steamers, and the faint and lonely sounds of the regimental orchestra's *Garry Owen*.

CAPTAIN CLARK'S
FISHING ACCESS

Abandoned Town of Waco, Montana,
Yellowstone River August

BROTHER MOON RISES above a cottonwood river bottom horizon. A mile away in the opposite direction, sandstone cliffs fringed with Ponderosa pine enjoy the last warm light of the sun.

The folding chair I've borrowed from the fire circle of companions is a foot away from the edge of a crumbling dirt bank where the river has done some serious damage this year. Water the color of dull jade moves past about fifteen feet below me, and I am separated by large blocks of pure sod that have already started their journey, either to another river island in the making or to the levees of New Orleans 3000 miles to the southeast.

The soft loam is defenseless against the remorseless whims of current. A small tree that recently lived on this bank is now largely submerged about fifty feet downstream; its branches sluice the flowing waters in a final loud chorus, creating the rhythms I will soon sleep with.

The old town, relatively speaking of such places in Montana, of Custer is giving an appreciation picnic for those who have helped support their small Junction City Memorial Park over the last year. Junction City was the hell-roaring frontier town across the river that Custer supplanted when the railroad chose the south side.

So now, between the time of the picnic and when we care to leisurely rise tomorrow, Bruce proposed a river float of sixteen water miles. He never goes anywhere in a straight line, preferring instead to meander to any point of interest he may imagine. He had wanted to stop at Pompey's Pillar National Monument Visitor Center on the way down here (down meaning down-river to me). I said I'd just meet him here. I didn't feel like pulling the river entourage into the Pillar's parking area and everybody dismounting for a tour. I was focused on the trip as planned. Probably a character defect I need to mend if I am to ever reach enlightenment—but not yet.

With the great convenience of cell phones, we all manage to stay connected, coordinated, and to actually meet at this fishing access and campground with the historical name. There is the Spaulding Family traveling first class thanks to daughter Pane with her new RV that has everything. Her large rubber raft, also first class, is on a trailer behind my old red Toyota pickup. The Spaulding group includes Pane, her sister Les, her dad and mom, and two nephews. James, the father, had ridden down with me. Not a lot of conversation there; two severely impaired conversationalists alone in a windy pickup cab. I can plead to having trouble hearing when the background buzz is the wind coming through rolled-down windows. James, too, probably.

WHEN THE SKUNKBRUSH TURNS

The waxing moon gets whiter as the evening sky darkens. I'm not sure if the river gets louder. Maybe it's just me wishing to lessen the noise of the disappointing neighbors I share the human race with—their portable generator, loud and stupid music, ringing cells phones, and boisterous conversation spiked with uproarious laughter after references to various parts of the female and innumerable ways to refer and discuss same.

I'm hoping the mosquitoes restrain themselves, as I want to sleep, not in my tent, but in the back of my truck, my head sticking out from the camper shell, resting on the tailgate and looking up at the stars and moon, listening to the sweet sounds of river and prairie night.

This area of Montana is near the center of the Indian Wars of nearly 150 years ago. I can almost see my great grandfather Henry leading a reconnaissance along the brush line; tall in the 3rd U.S. Cavalry saddle, having earned every chevron on his dark woolen blouse through campaigns from Apache to Sioux. The railroad whistle that soars through the night is the same that disturbed the Indians. Some of the rail line embankments constructed by Chinese workers over a hundred years ago, most of whom probably died in the long process of building the transcontinental rail, are still visible in places.

It's calm now, the evening maturing. Mosquitoes are small but still sting with who knows what new terrorist concoction of West Nile Virus, the green chigger shits, or whatever new has been imported to this once pristine land. Downriver a mile, the flash of a cell tower blinds. I'm waiting for technology to make them all obsolete.

My grandmother came here on a buckboard from New York and lived to see men walk on the moon. I should be able to outlive the freakin cell towers. Outlasting the rednecks is a millennium challenge.

The bothersome crowd next door has passed out, the river murmurs like a dream, Brother Moon dominates the sky, reflected now like a lily pad in the swirling waters of the night. The great stillness of prairie night descends and enwraps me in maternal arms.

It's morning. A tumble of still dark clouds lie low on the eastern horizon, above the reflecting meanders of the river. I've parked so I can both enjoy the dominance of the moon's journey as well as see the sunrise above the river. The top line of the tumbled clouds is iridescent. A brilliant red flare of new sun shoots through the lowest V in the cloud horizon and comes straight at me across the water. It seems magical, but it's probably a phenomenon available to any located where I am.

Sitting again above the river in the comfortable chair, the sun comes up to me from the water where its reflection is broken in constantly moving mirrors of the flowing water. Near the center of the river, the stream appears placid, disturbed only by undercurrents, feeding fish, and insects. I could move back aways from the sun's warm reflections on the skin of my old and susceptible face, but how many mornings of the year do I look down from my chair and see the green water pouring past me, speaking its ancient mantra. I'm reminded of Pete Seger's *Roll on Columbia.*

The temperature is in the seventies and the sun, though still not hot, has vanquished the mosquitoes. There is no wind. Do I deserve this?

Bruce crawls out of his tent into the sunlight and grins at me. It's going to be a good day on the Yellowstone River.

PLACE NORTH OF BILLINGS

THERE'S A PLACE north of the Heights—maybe the latter is called North Billings now—that is the last bastion of prairie rimrocks and pines, an outlander piece of land. About a half mile west of the Roundup Road, the area has remained off-track, probably due to its location in the middle of someone's active horse pasture.

I've always thought it would be a great place for a homesite if other homes could be kept away, and even dreamed of purchasing it somehow and placing it in a non-development conservation easement—except for my house, of course. Its only drawback is that the southern viewshed is the rapidly encroaching suburbs of the Heights, separated only by the Sindelar Shorthorn Ranch. The latter will eventually disappear as land values escalate.

The island of pine and rock has no access other than to park along Highway 87 somewhere and walk across the open space, feeling exposed to the possible ire of the unknown landowner and the eyes of the heavy traffic on that Redneck Highway. But one recent day of summer, wearing Tevas, sun shirt, and shorts and keeping an eye out for rattlesnakes, I do just that. It's my birthday and a present to myself. There's a whole mile-square subdivision of one-acre lots being carved into the prairie immediately north of the place, and I want to explore the small island of pine and rock before it's swallowed by new residents.

WHEN THE SKUNKBRUSH TURNS

I'm a prairie dweller and a prairie lover and to wander in among such places of pine and hoodoo is to walk in the cathedrals of God. It's a sanctuary for flycatchers and goatsuckers, magpies and mourning doves, meadowlarks and prairie sparrows. The beautiful cry of a red tail hawk echoes above me. In the swales, the sun is hot and the air still, while on the rises the sweat-cooling wind moves musically through the ponderosa and jack pine. The grasses, like on the flatlands, are golden crisp, the ground a fine dust that, at the end of day, will be in the corner of my eyes. The motionless profile of a cottontail's head against the sky on a small rim above me is worth a photograph. This small rabbit, near the very bottom of the local food chain, is abundant in the area, a good sign for the health of the wildlife residents here—and a meal promise to me when times harden. Gnawed pine trunks leave the presence of the bashful porcupine, cloved pointed tracks that of the deer.

Absáaloke oral history has the Crows of old seeking visions here, and I find a dim petroglyph on hard, south-facing sandstone, almost totally vandalized by at least thirty bullet holes. Other than this destruction, it is still clean here without the litter that is the evidence of man.

A small, old, white deer skull sits staring westward alongside a cattle path between the upper and lower rock areas, a sentinel of time, perhaps for time. A hoodoo stands mute testament to the continuous and ancient wind that still defines this land, and a broad, flat expanse of pure stone floor edged with the long needles of the ponderosa is all that remains of a sea millions of years in the past. A chickadee flits up, talking one of its many tongues; I am too dumb to understand. They have talked to me before, and although I know not their speech, I can grasp their attitude. Once their rapid staccato ire, directed at me for something I wasn't appreciating or doing properly, reminded me of paratroop sergeants long ago.

My cell phone chirps. I brought it with me for the ease of using its camera, but now it reaches up through the time warp here to touch me with Verizon. I smile. It's my daughter. I tell her I'm doing a birthday hike on the prairie. She understands.

Walking close to the base of one of the two rows of rimrock is to go where the small ones travel. The fine sand that blows in or erodes from the rock above displays the tracks of everything from bobcat to snake to ant lions and deer mice. I like to walk such places in winter when the Montana cold is tempered by the heat sink of deep sandstone and such pathways are usually bare of snow. It's then a good place to sit in the watery sunshine out of the winter wind and nap a few daydreams.

Although I think I can hear the anguish of the breaking prairie to the north where the heavy machines are carving roads and I can see the cars and trucks on the Redneck Road to the east, here it is quiet, and one has to still to listen for the wind carrying the bird melodies.

WHEN THE SKUNKBRUSH TURNS

I realize that this is what "recreation" means or is supposed to—the re-creation of one's soul.

To the west of the outcropping of this small prairie island, the scattered trees and sandstone give way to the vast undulating, lion-colored prairie; the skunkbrush sumac that accompanies the scattered remains of small sand rims will soon turn brilliant red like Christmas decorations in autumn. The summer birds will take their melodies to warmer places, and the magpies and ravens will mock them and man and will be here when we are long gone, leaving only the desolation of everything we created and touched.

CAL CUMIN

Muskrat Child

Bighorn River
muskrat child
poking me in the leg underwater.
Curious courage in a small heart
exploring
his prairie water home.
A brief touch of an alien world
like a time warp where
present and ancient blend
for a moment
At the end of a small
muskrat's nose.

RETURN[8]

IF IT HADN'T been for a pinched nerve making my right leg unreliable, I probably would have been wearing a silly grin, the one of just pure happiness that I get when I'm doing something I really enjoy. Today it's returning to a small pine and sandstone canyon to get some photographs I need for an article I wanted to complete.

Late November and it's seventy degrees, sunny, and with little wind. It doesn't get much better in Montana. I'd parked my old Toyota truck in the borrow ditch next to what just looks like a large, sagebrush-covered piece of flat prairie. The ditch should be called "dump" rather than "borrow" as assholes use these rural roads for disposal of everything from animal carcasses to old tires. Near my truck is not one but two loads of branches and wood chips, and there seem to be more beer bottles than the last time I visited.

The fence is neglected and I can step through, getting only one barbed wire snag in the back of my hoody. A black Angus bull is staring at me as I hobble along, and I pick up a piece of ancient fence post and carry it like a rifle; you never know what goes on in a damn bull's head.

---

8   First published in Last Best News, December 6, 2016.

The sun reflects off small stones scattered along the trail I'm following. I pick one up; it is smooth and thoroughly polished by some unknown process, usually about an inch in diameter, and slim, like a lozenge. When I was younger, I developed the theory that such polished stones were gizzard stones from ancient reptiles. Still works for me until I learn different. Makes them more interesting. I don't resist the urge to pocket several, not knowing what I will do with them at home, but like horse chestnuts, I can't resist massaging them.

I finally reach the end of the flat land and a canyon drops away below me, filled with mature ponderosa pine, juniper, and sandstone cliffs. The roots of long-dead monarchs protrude from seams in the cliffs and the carcasses of the ancient giants rot slowly into the sandy earth nearby.

In the bottom of the small valley there is still water sparkling in the sunlight, making me wish I had such a stream somewhere. I would fence at least a portion of it off from the destruction caused by cattle and nurture the wetlands that would blossom with all the traditional riparian species, maybe even invite a beaver or two. As it is now, the pockets of water I see are in the deep, muddy hoofprints of cows.

I proceed slowly down the steep hillside; my right leg definitely doesn't work unless I keep it straight. After one particularly loud groan, I see a large, dark mulie glide silently away in front of me, definitely worth a smile.

I also don't see other human footprints in the fine sandstone dirt, just those of deer and cattle. I know that there are a lot of other prints of the smaller animals, the mice, marmots, pack rats, and such that I can see better under the overhang of cliff where soft soil stays dry in south-facing shelter. This is old homestead country and I know I'm not the first to be here, but it's always nice not see recent waffle stompers in my path.

That illusion of relative solitude vanishes when I encounter survey posts and the track of the four-wheeler the surveyor used. The posts weren't here the last time I was, and I realize that what I'm seeing is a really large footprint—that of the suburbs, voraciously stepping out from the nearby city.

It's midday, but the shadows of early winter are long in front of me as I turn back toward my truck. The arc of the moon will be higher than this winter sun. Tomorrow is the full super moon of sixty-nine years ago. It would be wonderful to photograph it here in this magic little canyon silhouetted against tall pines and cliffs, coming up from the east, the direction this small drainage leads to the Yellowstone. However, trying to maneuver in darkness would be a disaster with a bum leg. I'll have to settle for photographs from my prairie porch, maybe Photoshop them later with pines and cliff.

A GUNMETAL TIME OF DAY

THERE IS A gunmetal time of evening after the sun has gone and before the gray of the twilight deserts into the darkness. It's a monochrome magic time that catches the last images of everything before each is swallowed by the deep dark of night. It's an alive time, defining for a few moments all that happened during the day. It allows one to sketch in memory the best of those bright daylight hours of life.

CAL CUMIN

THE BEWITCHING HOUR

THE BEWITCHING HOUR changes each evening, and it cannot be seen in a town or city. It happens on the prairie or, generally, in the country, and is that time of stillness when the landscape turns to complete darkness, but the huge sky above is gray, often with roiling clouds. It is a time between the ending day and overcoming darkness of night.

It is when the benevolent forces of darkness begin to clean, once again, the tarnished, tired shadows of the day, cleansing the bad, burnishing the good, and supporting the recuperative powers of the land. The latter still vibrant even as man seeks asunder, ruination, and profit.

Closing the book about wars I knew, plugging in the first disk of the complete set, seven seasons, of *Californication*. Watched them all previously and enjoyed their irreverence. Bought complete collection. Putting in the first disk this evening, hoping for refreshment from that damnable war.

After what I've been reading, the video series seems superfluous, shallow, bleached. I turn it off after the first session and sit in the darkness of this prairie spring evening. And sipping, too, Canadian Mist in triple doubles with creek water. Trying to reach the end of something—or enlightenment of some kind. Just sitting here, slightly leaning back in my desk chair. Hoping for succor from whatever source. Now am writing, bereft of succor, still, as always, wondering—what the fuck.

I know it will come, seemingly late in the day, but, still, the setting sun's gold spreads horizontally across the green prairie landscape. This is a prairie scenario, not the clouds and the great sky above, but the lusty sun and the clefted, undulating plains with the changing shadows. The latter long, my tallest pine reaching almost to a half mile away. Only a gentle breeze moves the twinkling cottonwood leaves, having ranted all day, it ushers in a cooler tomorrow.

CAL CUMIN

Sky

I am a student of sky and
old buffalo prairies,
of great tangling wisps of clouds
that mix well
the ghosts of vast herds and warriors
whose dust still lingers
in the stillness of summer evenings.

From horizon to far horizon
a faceted sky
gives coyotes the chance to step down into coulees
and winged antelope the wind
to run
from the platform of clouds.

The dark underbellies
of thunderheads
camouflage the sagebrush
and the scent of night
into which the shimmering
evening melts.

A vast lowering of cloud
goes to earth
at a far line of land, a path
in which the years
and millennium slip silently by.

WHEN THE SKUNKBRUSH TURNS

Pines silhouette against
the distant twilight
and, like Velcro, hold the lid
on awareness.

Crinoline patterns of fire smoke—
like bruises
and a creek leaks the light of sky
into an abyss of earth.

Distant virga drape
gray curtains
over a narrow slash of evening gold,
etching sandstone bluffs
like timeless signals to ancient herds
stirring in the gathering twilight.

The setting sun, distorted
oblong and orange
tries to hold its glory of the day
but, giving up,
is swallowed by the night.

CAL CUMIN

Sacrifice

It must have seemed very high
to the young warriors of the prairies
who blinded their horses
to ride there and die
the nearby bluff of pine and stone
was rich with the prayers
and bodies of their loved ones.

Sky and prairie challenge us
to do better,
to live up to something
ephemeral.

PRAIRIE WATER

THERE IS A shallow, water retention dam northeast of my place out on the sagebrush-covered prairie flatness. With all the rain and snow we've had this year, it is probably three times as large as normal. There is something magical about any water at all in this dry landscape.

It takes me forty-five minutes to hike to it, meandering around cactus and the leg-grabbing sage—watching the ground to avoid the serious cactus but also looking for arrow points and new flowers I haven't seen or identified before. In my five years out here, I've never found any archeological artifacts like points, although there are a lot of baculites and similar relatives around.

On my way back, I find a small, reddish-colored, broken point, and that makes my day. One of the notched edges is missing, as is the tip, but it's a great find. I look at it briefly and drop it in my pocket. Back home I will meditate on it and see what it will tell me, if anything. Sometimes I get wonderful images; sometimes nada.

I notice I tend to drift to my right as I hike and have to keep orienting myself on a distant tree line, glad I'm not in the middle of snowstorm or starless night. The cactus is almost ready to bloom, and I need to go back in a week or so to enjoy it. I Googled how to transplant the prickly pear and learned that the best way is to cut off the lobes and set them aside for a few days until they heal, then plant them, scar-side down. I wonder if any other plants require this rather weird procedure.

The most common flower is the purple, two-grooved milkvetch, and it's in pretty scrawny condition, in tune with the usually dry, gumbo land—also lots of death camas and wild onion. At the leaf base of the latter, it smells of onion, so it's a good identifier plus there is only one bulb; wild garlic—which looks similar—has a cluster of them. I use my Android to take pictures of the plants I'm not sure of. Back in my home office, I've taken apart two, used volumes of *Weeds of the West,* and separated the forbs by color, the easiest way for me to identify the myriad weeds; I'm still trying to figure out the grasses, which may be a lifelong pursuit.

I anticipated seeing either rattlers or bull snakes on this nice, warm, sunny day, but don't. The little prairie birds are both shy and quick, and I fail to see any long enough to identify and add to my prairie life list. As I near the water, I have to detour around the many small coulees that feed into the main body as they either contain water or mud. There are a few Canada geese on the water and other ducks that move quickly away as I approach. I see a couple of northern pintails and, in the distance that I don't approach, the large brown-bodied, white headed snow geese. At least that's what I think they are.

WHEN THE SKUNKBRUSH TURNS

I'm enjoying myself, but an old Army pain in my right knee is objecting to the warm weather and long pants I'm wearing, so I head home, still exploring the ground and enjoying the vast openness of the landscape. I had left my two old Dachshunds at home, favoring their short legs, age, and the prominence of cactus, and when I get back they act like I've been gone a week. After jumping up on my legs they race outside to sniff my backtrail to see what I've been up to.

CAL CUMIN

I have a full moon
watching over me at night
telling me dreams

relentless, the wind
worries trees and grass
like a hound on scent

WAITING FOR THE POISON TO WORK

I THINK THE bindweed in my yard is laughing at me. I can't call it a lawn; it's just a rural yard. Former owners tried landscaping with different colored rock separated by landscaping logs, pinned down, the rock underlain by black weed-proof mat, so they thought. Bindweed knows better.

It's almost a game at times. I grab a handful of it and rip it up, sometimes gently, trying for more root. I'll probably get ten different roots. Each one I break off, I've learned, comes back tenfold—rapidly. I'm trying to cover ninety percent of the yard with flat sandstone, serving both as a walkway across wet gumbo and a crusher of the damn weeds. I've started the process.

When I lift a piece of landscape rock that I positioned a month ago, I see the bindweed root, completely white, moving out to the edge of the rock, seeking light, and efflorescence—sometimes a foot away. Why can't agricultural science come up with a use for this tenacious forb; it could feed the world. Greens Are Us! Maybe there's a second career here. There's a lot of energy in that plant! I pull it by the handfuls and in a couple of weeks, I can do the same—no diminishment!

Okay, so the poor man's science lab, i.e., the internet, says it's edible. Now all that's needed is for one of those celebrity chefs to come up with something featuring bindweed in a big way, and we're off and running. Doubt if I can get any new trend applied to my damn yard, however.

I'll give it a try. Collect a bunch, not hard, and strip the leaves off, enough for a good-sized salad. Now what's needed is something tasty to separate the leaves so they're not all matted together. Chopped baby carrots should work. Gouda cheese. Bacon bits. Am I on a roll or what! Maybe include some bugs, insects ya know. Fry'em first to make them crunchy. Grasshoppers would be good, I think. Spiders are my roommates, so they're out, plus the idea of eating them makes me a little queasy. Same with beetles; I like them; they're cool. I have to look up how to cook grasshoppers, pull their wings off, fry'em alive, what?

As it is, with all the moisture we've had, the bindweed is even climbing the cheat grass. Would we could pair them off, winner take all, the other dies, and then we spray the damn survivor.

I am not a believer in herbicide, hate to support Dow and the other chemical industries for all kinds of reasons, not the least Agent Orange. Just another lie in the war of the same. My hand pulling, however, is tacking against the prairie wind. I am not an all-day, every day farmer-gardener—which is what it apparently takes even if you're not trying to raise anything, just trying to keep your head above the rapacious weeds!

Final action, mow, mulch, and bag it and put it in a compost pile, a pile that never works, but at least it contains the cubic yards of weed, cheat grass, and whatever else I can scoop up in my Honda multipurpose mower which "always starts." This is cheatgrass country—rust-colored acres after acre just waiting to plant another billion seeds in the vulnerable prairie. The abusive ranchers, the absentee landowners, the too-stupid-to-know-anything, the ninety-three percenters. Maybe combine it with my new friend bindweed? Bindgrass? Cheatweed? Needs to be catchy or eating America will never buy in. When we manage to screw our environment up so badly that traditional eating habits disappear, they will appreciate my cooking. Need to get a tome out: *Post- Apocalypse Dinner.* That's catchy.

CAL CUMIN

THE MOUSE

I SEE THE movement out of the corner of my eye from the perch at my desk, whiskey and creek water within easy reach, casually reading Luis Alberto Urrea's *Wandering Time*—again. Just enjoying his thread of conscious style and trying to feed my end of day brain something other than the usual dramatic fiction, with a spectacular spring evening outside except for the cold wind from mountain snowpacks still extant.

I know it was a mouse, but I'm a little surprised at its size; he or she is definitely healthy. He's halfway across the wide doorway into my office when he notices me turn my head in his direction. He scampers back to the mess of wood chips and miscellany behind my wood stove. I keep my eyes on the general area, noticing any movement. There is some. He's still there. Pretty soon, I see a mouse head in profile stick out from behind a picture frame on the floor. (I don't have any space left on my walls!) He's facing ninety degrees away from me, and I can feel his eyes surveying me in relation to the open space in front of him—the chances of a sprint of success.

I have a friend who writes children's books about a rodent character named "Junior Mouse." I feel like calling him and saying, "Come on over. There's a whole novel going on here."

WHEN THE SKUNKBRUSH TURNS

I know I live with mice. This is an old fixer-upper and they came with the title. Pack rats too, but I try real hard to limit them to the attached garage. I think I'm successful in that; however, this morning I noticed two weird gnawings in an apple I left on the counter last evening. I'm familiar with Mr. Bushy-Tailed Wood Rat from an earlier encounter. He was bold enough awhile back to sample several plums and apples on my counter and leave his distinct teeth marks before trying to carry away a large plum weighing more than he did.

I've found the most effective deterrent is a commercial grade, sonic doohickey that apparently is offensive to the little shits—mice and pack rats. I have one on the end of my kitchen counter. The sonic things are line-of-sight. In other words, anything blocks their deterrent beams—whiskey glasses, whiskey bottles, dirty dishes, etc. After seeing the ominous gnaw marks this morning, I cleaned off my counter, stuck my George Forman grill in a heavy-duty, plastic bag from some men's store and put it on top my fridge. I haven't seen any mouse turds up there, but I'm sure Sir Edmund Hillary Mouse will be there to soon enough.

I'm a great believer in not too much sterility in my environment. After working in the yard, dirt under my fingernails and grass stains on my hands, I have no compunction at all about fixing myself a sandwich without washing my hands. It's about connection to the Earth from which we are. Well, there is hoof and mouth disease, but there are no hooves around here. Paws for sure; no hooves.

Mr. Mouse is headed in the direction of my kitchen, but I think I'm ready for him. However, backed up to a kitchen counter is a convertible bed-couch that was here when I arrived at my great challenge. This is modern, open design—the kitchen next to the living room. The couch is not stained or dirty, not too, anyway. The biggest stain is some wax from a candle I unknowingly spilled on the side of it one cold winter evening. When I first unfolded the bed part, there were mouse turds on the thin mattress.

My daughter thinks I need a new mattress on my bed; she should see this assembly! Reminds me of Army beds, i.e., sleeping places, I have known—ponchos in the rain, concrete floors, bunker mud. I figure by now this hideaway bed, or whatever it's called, is probably a super sweet, mouse condominium complex. Probably that's where Mr. Mouse is going—home, kids, wife, TV, you know. I'm congenial. Stay away from my food. We'll get along. I think the mouse is my muse tonight. My two doxies are clueless.

ANOTHER EVENING

THE SUN'S GOING down in a glory blaze of cloud-scattered light. My little female doxy, Muki is snoring slightly, a purr that gives me pleasure in a sterile day. She's the smaller one with the widow's peak pattern on her forehead and the expressive, sensitive brown eyes. Like me now, she can't hear for shit (CHS), and I usually must catch her eye to get her attention. She likes to bark to go outside, and, I think, she feels she's performing some service to me and her younger brother Spike. She loves it when I respond, getting up from my desk and letting her out—along with Spike who's now also excited, much to Muki's pleasure.

She's always been, in the seven years since I retrieved them both from the shelter, the more independent one, seeking to find her own space rather than always being near me, as is Spike's preference. Lately, she's been warming up more, even taken to bouncing up and down on her hind legs in front of me which means, I think, that she wants me to pick her up. When I do—and hold her—she's very serious, looking at me, sometimes cautiously approaching my mouth with her skinny tongue, almost snakelike. Spike loves to slop all over my mouth and face if I'd let him, but Muki is appreciative of just a slight kiss. So am I.

Maybe I am a disciple of twilight. Not sure what it is that attracts me, maybe the pulling in of the shroud of nightfall, which both protects and insulates, comforting to me and my doggies. And then to go outside into the now quiet evening and piss off the porch, per Cactus Ed Abbey, and hear a meadowlark still calling for a new love and the disturbed mourning dove yelp in the ponderosa above me. Then to notice, way off to the northwestern horizon, the afterglow of the sun still searing the remains of the day. And then the darkness does come and all things on the land blend into the night as the sky above turns the darkest gray. As the gray deepens, the night itself spreads broadly across the land, stars begin their tiny glow, and the gray of Earth's late evening yields to the deep darkness of the galaxy.

The lights of distant towns, the cell towers, the headlights come on strong, more jarring than the billion twinkling stars above, but, I guess, one can think of either in his preference; mine is to the whirling Jupiter and the Evening Star and all of her brilliant and ever so distant entourage.

Now is the time of the coyotes to yell and yip. Even though I've lost much hearing, their joyous song can still echo in my head, a combination of memory and remaining ability. The parts I can't hear are now joined to those prairie songs of the past that have accompanied me on the rivers and prairies I've wandered.

Man cannot create the combination of clarity, joy, braggadocio, wildness, and exuberance of the song dog. It's his concert, rewritten every evening and sunrise, a gift to those of us who listen with our hearts, a challenge to those who hate him. I also feel a sadness and concern when I hear the sharp, clear call of the newly wandering offspring of this year; there is a questioning in his instinctive call, not sure what it will bring from the nearby houses. And yet, he or she still calls, slightly forlorn, a touch nervous. I hope he survives, at least to have a family before my fellow man blows him away.

A fully-grown, rusty-colored coyote visited me last summer. Shouldn't say "visited," I guess; he was just going somewhere, and me, transfixed at my office window, mentally urging him to hurry across the pasture below me before some redneck pickup driver shot him. He didn't even pause in his jaunt when he caught an unwary vole, tossed it up in the air, and swallowed it, continuing on. I would love to know where, to whom, and doing what. He's smart. They are smart generally. They have to be; there are more rednecks with long rifles than there are of them.

The big cats wander through here occasionally, down various coulees from the pine-covered rimrocks three miles to the west. I feel sorry for them; it must be very hard to live with humans who fear and kill them at will. Where does a hundred and eighty-pound cat curl up in the day? Their five-inch paw tracks in the spring mud are startlingly wonderful. I keep my two doxie buds close in the darkness; they would attack in Dachshund hubris, afraid of nothing until rolled and taken.

All afternoon, the rain clouds gather and, in the evening, the rain comes, just enough to melt the gumbo and trap me to the gravel around my house. Then, late in the May evening, the sun bursts out in the west as the rain clouds move eastward. I have to get up, go outside, and see it—to keep the purity between my eyes and the misty sun. It's worth it, of course. A huge rainbow, like a large Quonset hut opening, frames the eastern horizon. Nothing grandiose, just a rainbow.

There remains only a shallow dribble from the day's whisky, and, as I swish around in my mouth, it disappears. Brother Moon is being enveloped by the forces of nightfall, his pearly face becoming misty in the clouds.

Gray clouds, gray night, the subtle gray of female sparrow breast. As the Monkees wrote and so beautifully sang, "I see the world in a different light/things not always black and white/through all these years still, to this day/My hardened eyes see only shades of gray."

SUMMER STORMS

I LOVE SUMMER storms on the prairie. I can see them coming thirty miles away, the storm pods luminescent and the rain making silvery streaks to the ground. The best is the lightning and thunder, although my two doxies fear it and want me to hold them—which I appreciatively do.

I must be careful with the recently replaced screens on my winter-bare windows. The former, opened wide, tend to accumulate debris, both inside and out. Some plastic packing material keeps rising to one screen, the pressure of the wind inside pushing the flimsy screen out. I pull it from the screen and put it on the floor only to have it leap back and cling to the screen again. Finally, I put it on the floor and put the plaster cast of Yellowstone Wolf No. 21's paw prints on it to hold it down. From the storm side, the open window screens collect bits of leaves, bugs, and grass, and it's easier just to close the window to stop the collecting.

The heat of the eighty-plus degree day is slowly draining from my humble old trailer house add-on home.

Respectful of the plunging strikes of lightning, I shut down my computer.

I had made some space in my rain storage tanks for new stuff, but the most effective gutter over my sliding glass doors is apparently plugged, as evidenced by the rain pouring from it onto my porch and the lack thereof coming out of the spout to the storage tank. I wish I could analyze all the small living things that are accumulating in that tank! Without a pressure washer, these opaque, white polyethylene tanks are difficult to clean, and, every year the water gets greener.

After the relative violence of the storm, it becomes completely calm and the temperature drops slowly, but it is the smell of the prairie showered clean with rain that enchants, a smell so unique, honest, and earthy that I know it's one of the reason I live out here on this gumbo hill.

Shortly, I will need to get up and close some of the post-storm windows, leaving wide open those in my bedroom where my doxies and I can burrow under my still-winter down, and face off the thirty-plus temperature of the night. I also know, with the windows open tonight, I will taste that rain scent all my dreaming hours.

The sun has emerged in the west through the storm-mixed sky and the shadows are long. The meadowlark's sharp and distinct call is clear and loud in the post-storm quiet. If my old ears could hear better, I know there are Says phoebes, starlings, black birds, and numerous families of sparrows out there also singing their simple enjoyment of the evening rain and the succor of the setting sun.

WHEN THE SKUNKBRUSH TURNS

The storm clouds above that brought the rain and wind are breaking up, each distinctive in its dissolution. Some have caught the direct brilliant rays of the setting sun and responded in giant appreciation of pink splendor. Others are massaging into blue-grayness as if wondering where to go, what to do with their short-lived, violent finery. The high color in the clouds to the east that have carried the storm away is not the soft pink of ending day but fiery red inside high billowing cumulous; their mission is not yet complete on the old buffalo prairies.

What's remarkable is the stillness. Wind here on the prairie is a given, and when it pauses for however long it is like a background noise that suddenly stops—and you notice, not before, but when it stops, its absence.

It allows, for one thing, all surrounding sounds to come suddenly to my damaged ears and not just those upwind from me, like the traffic from the Red Neck Highway west of me with its Harley noise machines.

Drinking the sweet Canadian whiskey, the choice for a now-forgotten reason. Probably the pain in the lower back and just getting freaking tired of feeling it—and the frustration of not knowing how to relieve it. My ass is sore; my lower back's gone to hell, making me gasp when I stand up. Then there is probably the usual weakness of the alcoholic. Like with the simple correct posture of sitting, I don't know the correct parameters of dealing with it all.

The eloquent meadowlark song comes clearly through the open windows. Muki's laying on the maroon leather couch, practically blending into the cushions, so totally comfortable and at home. I want to get up, go over, and kiss her lovely snout, but her nose is one of her private parts and she doesn't like it touched—same with her feet.

The wind comes up now, about thirty knots and jumping around, the seed heads of cheatgrass, Spanish bayonet, and Japanese clover are dancing. My hearing sucks so much I can't hear them singing. A drape of gray clouds impedes the sunset, the temperature has cooled, windows close.

In between the high brightness where the light of space still shines, the dark areas slowly expand where evening and night happen. The hunted and the hunter, the flowers and the weeds, and the antelope watch me warily with their ancient eyes. The old ones among the Crow, the Absáalokee, call this time of the year, "The moon when leaves are showing." I think I'll call it the "Time Before June," my favorite month. The gumbo has given up its deep frost from the cold winter past, as well as the recent rain. The surface is now dry, parched as only gumbo clay can suddenly be. The Bewitching Hour is past, blackness claims the land for a while, and the blanket of gray covers the land.

In the morning, when I retrieve my newspaper as the sun comes over the distant horizon in a molten ball, the rain scent and the new sun will create magic, nonpareil.

WHEN THE SKUNKBRUSH TURNS

it falls quietly
this rain of early summer
words we cannot hear

DAY ON THE TONGUE RIVER

I SAID THE flowering yellow plant thick along the gravel road was wild mustard. Dick said no, it was skeleton weed. Bruce's 82-year old mother said it sure was pretty.

We were being ferried back to our base camp below the Tongue River Reservoir Dam near Decker. Mick and Dick had been kind enough to drive the one-hundred and thirty miles down from Billings to enjoy part of our two-night camp and to ferry Don and Bruce's pickups to the get-out point. The latter seemed in contention for a while this morning when Mick decided, at the last minute, to try and change Bruce's carefully planned takeout. While staying out of the argument, it seemed to me we were either being picked up in three hours or at nine miles downriver.

When one is on a stream like the Tongue today, in a beautiful Souris River Canoe (Earl's), plenty of cold Keystone Light in the cooler, and ripe tomatoes with salad dressing (Earl's idea of lunch), mundane concerns like where and when we are being picked up are not all that important.

The storied Tongue, now tamed by a Montana Department of Natural Resources flood control dam, is high and fast today—and beautiful, gleeful in its springtime race to the Yellowstone River at Miles City. From our campground just below the dam, the roar of water vet-ted through the dam structure and the fresh snowmelt from the Bighorn Mountains to the south coming over the high spillway create a subtle, constant background roar day and night. Maybe it's camping under the lip of a couple million cubic feet of water, but, every once in a while, a wind shift would suddenly bring the roaring sound louder, causing one to glance quickly at the high wall of a still standing dam for reassurance.

After a leisurely and delicious breakfast prepared by Don beside a small fire (eggs, sausage, potatoes, onions, and other tummy stickers) plus a barrel of coffee, much of the latter from the elegant coffee press Pat'd fished brand new (she says) out of a Dumpster, we launch. The Tongue River Canyon is narrow, compared to the Yellowstone, and the lush green lands we pass are part of big ranches owned by either doctors or the Mars Candy Company. The machinery of large irrigation systems can be seen along the banks; although now dormant, they will suck this proud little river almost dry later in the summer.

The elegant head of a mule deer, with its ubiquitous splayed ears, follows our progress from the tall grass and shrubs. Cattle graze luxuriously in bright green hay fields. A large bull snake's swim in the river is rudely interrupted by our canoes and kayaks. Hand-sized mussels occasionally glisten from the bottom of the water. A large island forces our group to single-file down a narrow, green side-channel where the junipers, Russian olives, willows, and ponderosa pine arch elegantly over-head for our passing. An old road trail is gouged into the riverbank on each side, a low water ford that proba-bly contains old wagon tracks in its dusty memory.

A red tail hawk, or, as Bruce refers to it, the "Buick Bird," calls overhead; a bald eagle lumbers off its senti-nel branch, climbs closely up the scoria-colored hillside, and disappears over a small saddle in the ridge line. The wide variety of ducks seem shy, rising well ahead of us, making identification difficult and forcing one to watch the flight patterns and listen closely to the varied calls for any attempt at recognition. One group sounds like killdeers as they rise from the water. Ducklings and goslings frantically try to keep up with nervous parents just trying to get past us—or vice versa.

When Bruce and I had first driven down the valley and come to the very edge of the river, it was like "Whoa! This is so beautiful!" There are no guardrails or fences along the red and dusty road, and one can almost reach out the truck window and touch the beckoning river itself. Neither of us has changed our opinion.

Don tries yodeling; we think. Pat suns her legs on the gunnels of Don's canoe; Gary, in his nimble Dagger kayak, flits around us, passing a beer here, a tomato or jerky there between various craft. Bruce is in heaven, just sitting and absorbing the river scene from the mid-dle of his pretty, red We-no-nah canoe. It's his birthday.

WHEN THE SKUNKBRUSH TURNS

Maybe that's it. Rosemary and husband Dick slip effort-
lessly through the water in a 30-year-old tandem Folbot
kayak with original, matching paddles that haven't been
replicated for decades. Behind me, Earl grunts occasion-
ally and chuckles his pleasure of the day.

We'd come down the previous day to leisurely camp
and take our time getting on the river this morning,
to enjoy the red- black- and yellow-scoured hillsides,
colors created when the vast swamps of the Pleistocene
had burned. Under huge cottonwoods, the evening plan
was splendid in its implementation as the fire, beer, Pat's
stew, Jim Beam, conviviality, and total lack of mosqui-
toes maxed the good-times scale. Through the open,
unscreened door of my tent, Cassiopeia circled the polar
star through the quiet night. In the five a.m. light, I
learned that a few harmless centipedes, stone flies, and
moths had joined me in the warmth of my tent, but
nothing disturbed the serenity that now prepared the
clear and pale emerald sky brightening over the near-
by rim. The sun settled in the narrow canyon of the
Tongue slowly and inexorably, the heavy dew and night
chill melting in the new summer's heat.

A chorus of bird song spilled from the trees and brush
around us, some calls so loud it was almost painful to
hear. Even the starling mob was upstaged by the red-
wing blackbirds, tree swallows, and various warblers
and finches, although the croak of the occasional great
blue heron stood out. A house wren decided to serenade

me no matter how close I got to her perch in a small tree by my tent. Her delight in repeatedly singing her verse with its soft burr in the middle shook her whole body. Like the professional she is, she was giving it everything she has. The photograph I took of her will go on my screen saver, a reminder of her joy and of simple things. When the individual birds surrounding us were not singing, they flitted through the air, all seeming to have mouthfuls of food or fiber. We humans should be so composed—to work so hard, to be able to survive, and to sing our hearts out for the living community around us.

The Fish, Wildlife and Parks guys drive up. I wonder if they take courses in conviviality, as they seem to love to talk and visit. The whole, huge camping area of the reservoir above us is full—white with RVs and boats. The young wardens say it's pretty quiet, with "no large groups of kids looking for excitement."

With darkness the cacophony of birdsong will stop, replaced with the soothing, wet sounds of close-by river water moving along the willow-lined bank, down to the Yellowstone, on to the Missouri and Mississippi, and down to the great ocean mother. I want to say, "Hold it! Stay with us here awhile longer." This precious, quickly passing water fills our aquifers, irrigates our narrow valleys, provides for the prehistoric paddlefish miles to the north, fertilizes the Red River Valley, carries the heavy iron barges of the Mississippi, glides through huge cities, slips through the steamy flatlands of the Louisiana Delta, enters the stormy Gulf to be again absorbed in the maelstrom of creation that will eventually bring the moisture back to us.

It's easy to sink into subliminal, mystic worlds, sitting on a stump alongside a sparkling river, early on a late spring morning in Montana.

LATE RIVER AND
TWO MOON PARK

IN LATE WINTER mornings, the light comes sooner and stays longer, but there is still a kind of breathlessness in the still hours. It's as if the day doesn't yet know what to do with all the new hours, and the light is held in almost dream-like abeyance.

By midafternoon, the day is warming, however, and the ice has thinned along the river bottom backwaters. The water is clear and deceptively clean looking where the ice has pulled back, the drowned leaves of last fall's die-off and last summer's grasses lie peacefully on the clear bottom. On the bank I walk, the top layer of soil is no longer frozen, and the gravel along the water is loose once again and cascades as I walk down the steep bank.

Because of my habit of carefully watching where I walk, the ground reveals river history in the small pieces of civilization among the gravel that I still assess for good slingshot stones. A piece of red tile with a striated pattern ground down to the size of a quarter; a piece of brick crumbles away; a piece of glass from long-ago elixirs slowly turning purple, its sharp edges dulled by years in the roiling bottom of the river. Faded yellow plastic from an old shotgun shell rests among goose droppings resembling the burned ash of cigarettes. A new, dark red, foot-high crop of sandbar willows covers the narrow beach of a changeling island promising additional color, additional shelter, additional parkland. The beaver have harvested riverside trees, felling most of them straight toward the water. I wonder if the ones that fell in contrary directions earned the four-legged, nighttime contractor any comments from his peers.

An early pair of gnats swarm before my eyes, startling me because it's still cool. The river smell of dampness and decay and all the life crammed into the bottomlands mixes in remembrances of rivers past. I climb over the sand island, and the river itself greets me. There's no ice on it now. In the eddies, clumps of suds indicate the alien nutrients being added by the city just upstream, and, in a shaded backwater, waves lap a brown, grimy, lip of foam on an edge of old ice to drive the point home. I cross another low place where all the water has disappeared into a covering of defeated looking ice now draped over the soft contours of the barren land.

As I turn back inland, I stop and take a picture, listening to the way the river stillness delineates the city sounds from Lockwood across the way. My stillness makes some hidden whitetails nervous and they get up from their hiding places and bound toward the park. I turn quickly and retrace my steps, hoping I haven't driven them into the main park area and the maws of the mastiff darlings let loose there. The white tails probably lead the mutts in circles, but I wonder what happens when the deer have offspring hidden in the brush the dogs mindlessly charge through.

The wide placid water of the winter river narrows into small fast currents where its soft susurration increases in volume. Just before the wide plain of water loosens itself to plunge into the small, narrow cascade, it changes subtly, a smooth, sensuous undulation hugging for just for a moment the stillness of its own perfection. In the deepest part of the rushing narrows, the bottom stones disappear, and the water becomes an opaque green, a color lightened by the pale blue of sky and whiteness of clouds. Some goldeneyes and mallards keep their distance, watching me, floating effortlessly ahead.

The mainstream of high water has been carving each year the high bank I now walk on. In late spring, the river makes its own boundaries. The bank underbelly is soft and, as the rushing water comes, it yields easily to the greedy current, the dirt allocated to other land, the sand and gravel loosened to slide into the rushing water. I've always been fascinated by the roots left exposed by the taking of the soil: roots uniquely designed by rocks.

I leave the riverbank drawn by a contrast of golden heads of a tall grass against the gray underbrush a short distance inland. I follow a game trail, and, when I emerge to the small interior grassland, I guiltily brush hound's tooth burs from my Levis, knowing the tenacious little seeds will plant themselves and produce a full crop of new weeds. Our culture definitely needs to spend more time analyzing the survival traits of noxious weeds and less on such venues as the mating habits of pop divas.

WHEN THE SKUNKBRUSH TURNS

I'm not able to identify the beautiful grass nor do I learn why it grows there in such bright array. Maybe it's just part of the natural palette offered to those who notice.

This isn't a scientific expedition. It is just a chance to see The River and Two Moon in pre-spring ensemble. It is a time when winter is relaxing its hold, water still lies in the ruts and shaded ravines, and the smooth dirt trails are muddy and filled with dog tracks, a cold humidity the main essence. The Eskimos have many words for snow. We need more words for the murals of Montana's constantly evolving seasons. This one is a time just before promise.

CAL CUMIN

RED NECK HIGHWAY

MONTANA HIGHWAY 87 between Billings and Round-up: I call it the Red Neck Highway, and I live next to it—unfortunately downwind. So, the roar of all the freaking Harleys and the jacked-up pickups with their huge knobby tires can be heard coming and going for miles. I'm a sincere apostle of the concept that no one should be allowed to make noise that can be heard by anyone else more than ten feet away. In these wonderful "Me! Me! Me!" times, however, good luck with that one.

I don't know if 87 is trashier than most rural Montana roads, but, because I live here, I'm beginning to think it is. I'd hate to have to believe that all the roads in our beautiful state get trashed like this one. I think the assholes have discovered that when you throw your Budweiser cartons, paper coffee cups, and, of course, anything plastic in the back of your pickup in Roundup that, by the time you get to Billings, the truck bed is miraculously empty! And vice versa as the dumb bastards haven't learned that anything that floats at seventy miles an hour tends to leave the ole pickup truck.

Most notable in this latter category is paper, of course, but every day seems to bring new surprises. Once it was a carton full of Styrofoam paper plates. You talk about something that covers some territory when it's windy and that stands out against the prairie landscape, that debacle sure did. An eyesore that will last for our grandchildren to witness and question, hopefully; they will wonder anyway.

A couple of days ago some asshole put his Walmart necessities in the back of his truck including a huge carton of bum wad. It ended up scattered along the road. I think someone picked those up. I mean even Red Necks sometimes wipe their dumbasses. I just shook my head. Picking up their shit in front of my place keeps me plenty busy, leading even to having to purchase commercial garbage collection services. I could personally get by without paying for that, as I generate very little waste at my place.

Two days after the bum wad white out on the road, probably the same dumb ass lost a load of white paper towels. I mean, what do Red Necks need paper towels for? Maybe because his first attempt at using toilet paper had failed for mysterious reasons, he thought bigger and better things might work. Who knows?

I admire the volunteers who regularly come out and patiently pick up the litter along the borrow ditches. I wonder sometimes, though, if it doesn't encourage some of the lazy bastards who just throw whole garbage sacks full of their shit out the window, or, again, just leave it in the back, knowing it will float away. I always honk when I pass the volunteers, hoping they know it's a small thank you. I can just imagine the stuff these guys who volunteer a lot find.

Just across my quarter mile of frontage, I've picked up everything from mechanic's tools to a nice zippered sunglass case full of hypodermic needles. I rather doubt the latter find was something tossed on purpose, and I hope the freak who lost it had a serious case of withdrawal way back up in the hills where he dug his hovel.

Once found a plastic bag containing four cans of sardines with some kind of government stamp on them. They were unopened among fast-food wrappers.

And get me started on roadkill! The Salvation Army could feed the poor in the whole city with the meat that dies out here. Some of the poor animals can't be avoided. The big tractor-trailer rigs can't help but hit the animals that jump out ahead of them, but you have to wonder about all the rest of the charnel. You can usually see where metal and tissue impacted by the spray of blood on the pavement.

When that blood is on the edge of the road, it usually indicates Bubba swung out of the travel lane to nail the little sucker. I heard one Red Neck brag how he saw a rattlesnake by the side of the road, slammed on his brakes in his F-250, grabbed his handy .44 magnum, jumped out, and was only stopped when his dad (and I'm using that term charitably) yelled at him that the ricochet could drill his beloved truck. Bubba changed positions and proceeded to eviscerate the innocent snake before cutting off its tail to show the barmaid back at the Dew Drop Inn beer joint on the way home.

Because coyotes and me have some sort of weird mystical thing going, I always pull over and try and scrape what's left of them from the road, placing them gently in the borrow pit where the sun will find them. I know it's dumb, but you never know who or what is watching, and a man needs every point he can accumulate on his side of the ledger of life. Pity the poor bastard who enjoys running over the cottontails and the random killing of almost everything within the sights of some of his toys. I sincerely hope that the karmic furies of fate will catch up with him someday and give his dreams the split second of truck and tissue impact on a regular basis.

I stopped one day and pulled, as I couldn't lift, a large boar badger out of the centerline; he was beautiful, and I wish he had been my neighbor somewhere close so I could daily appreciate him and his life. Yesterday it was a big raccoon who appeared very healthy, and I wondered what he was doing way out here and what he was having for dinner to be so fat. I forgot to turn on my emergency blinker when I hopped out of the car to go to him, and the Red Neck flying by was probably thinking I was hide hunting.

Rabbits seem to get creamed the most, and I have to admit they're totally ignorant about the result of trying to dodge a Red Neck at seventy mph. Deer and antelope also seem pretty regular on the gore highway. I watched a cow elk try and get through several fences before she made it safely across ole 87, much to my relief. Then someone told a neighbor that he had seen a cow and two calves in the area, and I'm left wondering what happened to the two little ones. Probably, some good ole boy just shot them for pure "sport." Would the day come that I was king and could decree that all such hunters turn in their killing toys and become the hunted.

Walking to the mailbox, a prairie dog was trying to hide nearby, and I hope he can establish a new colony out here on my land; it's not good for anything else, and I like those cute little shits. But then, I also like the deer mice I find daily in my five-gallon bird seed bucket in the tool room. I have some sort of sonic devices in my kitchen that seem to keep the little critters away, but my tool room is separate. I harvest them each day and hope it's not the same wise guys, because I take the pail out to the barn and turn them loose.

I don't even want to get started on my western wood rat, aka: pack rat. But another time.

CARBON COUNTY VALLEY

THE ROAD CROSSES the bottom of a small valley. I pass a Realtor's "For Sale!" sign, quickly glancing away, trying to control what enters my brain, trying to avoid negative thoughts on this beautiful day of rolling green hills and large, slow-moving snowy clouds against a sky so clear and blue it reminds me of a fake sapphire I was once conned into buying in Thailand.

This little valley beckons me, however, extending on both sides of the road as far as the gentle hills that pattern the horizon let me see. A whole valley for sale, I'm thinking; how sad and rare because this little piece of Montana is not one of the grand Ted Turner acquisitions or a famed Stillwater River enclave attracting a Mel Gibson. I'm miles from anywhere and any urban sprawl but not far enough or fast enough to avoid the real estate business. As I drive up the valley toward the not too distant Beartooth Mountain Range that hovers over everything here, I savor the plebian joys of this still largely virgin piece of land.

My old Saab's driver's side window is down and a timeless smell of prairie grass carried in the wind centers me. Black Angus, some white-faced, are scattered along the valley's hills and occasional creek bottom. Recent rains have greened the slopes, and there is actually water glinting in the ancient streambed. This is the time of year the sales pictures are made and the Californians invited to visit Big Sky Country. This year the timing is critical because the drought is seven years old, and the green disappears like the dreams of innocents.

Those of us whose roots are generations deep in these high plains appreciate the barren, freezing winters that blow only a skiff of snow across the hills, the exposed ground as hard as rock, the yellowed bunch grass brittle as glass. The cold days are the price paid for the days like today, and both sit comfortably in my mind. It's the newbies who leave the silence of the cold for California, Arizona, and other southern familiarities.

They will never know the simple joy the early sun's warmth or the bleak, watery sunrise first peeking over the shattering cold built during an endless northern night. One appreciates life more from under the covers of a down comforter, thick hand-made quilt, or a richly haired mountain goat hide when the ice creeps across the bedroom window glass in exotic patterns from an alternate reality. Thank you, God, for all I have, including this Montana home, the sheer luxury of my warm and comfortable bed, and the protection of my frail human ass from the devils of the nether regions of deep Montana winter.

In a dry valley for eleven and a half months of the year, the trees and shrubs are scattered, judicious with the available water, and still standing against the drastic temperature changes and the depredation of the cattle.

WHEN THE SKUNKBRUSH TURNS

They are just enough to break the rhythm of the slopes, one after another up the valley. The range hasn't been abused, testimony to the probable fact that the descendants of the original homesteaders still work the ranch. Native grasses and forbs comprise the ground cover, the introduced carnivore species of usually Asian or European extraction are still not flagrant along the roadway.

The long, narrow valley has a sense of itself. It is what it is without apology. Redwing blackbirds nest in the hints of streambeds; sparrow hawks watch their territories from the highest points available. Shy songbirds of common colors sing their subtle differences into the clear early evening. Cottontails seem to want to hide but test their camouflage, crouching just beyond reach. Where the small rabbits are plentiful, the predators gather, reflecting the good health of the timeless cycle of supply and demand, and life and death that seems to only change or shift with the advent of the biped's blitzkrieg development.

One can tell this verdant valley is still a distance from the five-acre ranchettes that will soon inundate any place with a view or a few trees, to say nothing of beautiful small valleys—there are no Russian olive trees! This gray, sagebrush-colored invader is ubiquitous in any areas where the settled density is more than ten people per square mile.

Montana legislators, apparently bowing to the organization and power of an exploding real estate industry, exempted five-parcel land splits from most of the requirements of the state subdivision law. Ninety percent of the subdividing in Montana now avoids public hearing, environmental assessment, and parkland set asides. The real estate interests apparently also made sure that local residents couldn't put any other requirements into the state subdivision law that might be necessary for local conditions; any inclusion of local common sense not already required by the state is illegal.

Local residents, like myself, who have heard so much about the overpowering regulation of land are mystified when a new subdivision is proposed that is an abomination to the land they know intimately. All they hear is how land planners and local governments are preventing private landowners from the just use of their land.

Only the health and sanitation rules that require a minimum of one acre of land for combined water wells and septic tank drainfields hold the parcelization of the land at short sword abeyance. And for this bare minimum oversight, the Republican governor cut funding for the reviewing state agencies. However, this reduction in staff also has slowed down the subdivision approval process. This in turn infuriated the real estate industry further which in the next Legislature, made sure that mandatory processes have specific time limits; if they don't, then the proposed developments have a right to be done regardless.

If it didn't do so much damage to an ancient and beautiful land, it would be humorous black comedy.

But in a land where the whiskey roads carved by wooden carts a hundred and fifty years ago still show, the slash and burn developers with their large track hoes, backhoes, and dirt movers leave a landed disruption that will be our state's heritage forever. Huge industry feeds off the real estate development process like suckerfish off a blue whale.

Recently at a City-County Planning Board meeting in Laurel, a small community of seven thousand souls nestled in the fertile Yellowstone River Valley, a developer who neighbors said had created an instant disaster with his first subdivision proposed a second subdivision next to the original. Neighbors of the mess testified before the board at the requisite public hearing that the place resembled a garbage dump with kitchen and bathroom appliances strewn everywhere. One gentleman said the whole area bred rats that considered the place home. The landowner had carved, on his own accord, a fifteen-foot channel in the land in an attempt to make sewage drainfields. Adjacent neighbors complained about the impact of this new drainage canal on their own water table, but the biggest complaint was that the canal had become the convenient common garbage pit for the new subdivision residents. It was filling with garbage, destroyed furniture, and even an automobile. Downwind from the subdivision, the old sheep fence caught the plastic bags, fast food wrappers, Styrofoam, and everything else that society deems disposable—literally: out the window!

Needless to say, the neighbors did not want this mess expanded. The Laurel planner had to explain to the angry crowd that the Legislature limited what could and could not be approved. Bottom line, he said: landowners have a right to do pretty much what they want with their land—especially if they just promise to do better. This smoke and mirrors approval process then puts the whole issue on future enforcement by government agencies that are facing budget cuts.

By the time of the next Legislature, the neighbors will have resigned themselves to the bullshit of the local planning process—or moved elsewhere, and the real estate industry will keep fine-tuning the whole process in their undying attempt to maximize monetary return at the expense of everything else—a beautiful state, a fragile land, and a basic and common morality.

MONTANA FALL

FALL, AND NO matter how hot the daytime temperature gets and how sunburned your face can still get, the coolness of coming winter lurks in the shadows.

Sitting in the open area by the sliding glass door to my south-facing patio, one leg propped on the table, I am luxuriating in what may be the last hot days of this relatively cool Montana summer. Desiccated, yellowing leaves are dropping from the honey locust, and the breeze is dry and hot coming through the open doors. The wasps are enjoying the heat, and offspring of a beautiful orb builder spider has created a smooth round hole of tight webbing in the corner of the doorway. Junebugs laze on the hot walls and the glass panes of the doors.

I've clipped the tops of my potted tomato plants and nipped the latest blossoms. It will be a race now for the green bulbs to ripen before the sunlight hours shorten and winter's cold commandeers the patio.

I've started filling the bird feeder again to help some of my bright-eyed, feathered friends migrate the thousands of miles their instincts demand of them. So far, stay-the-winter chickadees are enjoying the seeds the most, while house finches seem to think my bird water is a Roman bath as ten skitter through the water at once.

CAL CUMIN

There are not a lot of other things a city condo dweller like myself has to do to get ready for the cold season. Move whatever potted flowers and vines one desires to save, inside, sweep the summer's debris from the deck, store the planters, and place the birdseed bin conveniently. Maybe clean the windows one last time, shining them up with the vinegar and water formula Mom used and hope the dust storms are over for the summer. The firewood collection is adequate, the fireplace cleaned, and the mats in the doorways ready for the coming mud and snow.

And even though it's almost ninety degrees, it's not as much fun to sit in the shade now as it was in mid-summer. The instinct is to savor the heat, absorb it—a primal urge from man's dim past when home and protection were a south-facing cave high enough to see the approach of danger and storm.

I have another glass of Sharptail Pale Ale. It's Sunday afternoon and hot. It won't taste quite as good when there's snow on the deck.

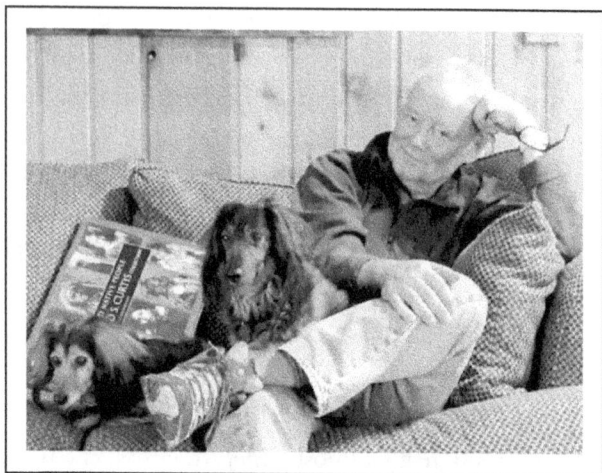

photo by Kay Foster

CAL CUMIN LIVES and writes from his home on the prairie west of Shepherd, Montana, not far from his Billings birthplace. This book of essays was inspired by his wanderings, his deep knowledge of Montana past and present, and his love of the land he calls home. Cumin, who spent most of his career as an independent land-planning consultant, lives with two long-haired dachshunds, Muki and Spike. The other lights of his life, his daughter and her family, make their home in Billings. She played a key role in bringing these essays to light.